DOMINICUS GUNDISSALINUS

THE PROCESSION OF THE WORLD

(DE PROCESSIONE MUNDI)

Dominicus Gundissalinus

THE PROCESSION OF THE WORLD

(*De processione mundi*)

TRANSLATED FROM THE LATIN
WITH AN INTRODUCTION AND NOTES

by

JOHN A. LAUMAKIS

MARQUETTE
UNIVERSITY
PRESS

Library of Congress Cataloging-in-Publication Data

Gundissalinus, Dominicus, 12th cent.
   [De processione mundi. English]
  The procession of the world / by Dominicus Gundissalinus ; translated
from the Latin with an introduction and notes by John A. Laumakis.
       p. cm. — (Mediaeval philosophical texts in translation ; no. 39)
Translation of: De processione mundi.
Includes bibliographical references (p.   ) and indexes.
   ISBN 0-87462-242-5
  1. God—Proof, Cosmological—Early works to 1800. 2.
God—Attributes—Early works to 1800. I. Laumakis, John A., 1972-
II. Title. III. Series.
  B765.G983 D413 2002
  212—dc21

                              2002153484

MARQUETTE UNIVERSITY PRESS
MILWAUKEE

The Association of Jesuit University Presses

For Peg and Jack,
Steve, Pete, Paul, and Mark,
and especially you, my Juliana

Table of Contents

Introduction

I. Gundissalinus's Life and Works

During the twelfth and thirteenth century, Christian thought in the Latin West was profoundly influenced by the works of ancient Greek philosophers—in particular, Aristotle—and by the Arabic works of medieval Muslim and Jewish philosophers, such as Avicenna, Averroes, Avicebron, and Maimonides. These Greek and Arabic philosophical works, however, could affect the thought of Christian philosophers and theologians in such a significant way only because, over the course of many years and at different locations throughout Western Europe, these works had been translated into Latin. The most important site for the translation of Greek and Arabic philosophical works into Latin was Spain, where the famed 'School of Translators of Toledo' was established by Archbishop Raymond of Toledo (1126-1151).[1] Although the 'School of Translators' flourished in Toledo well into the thirteenth century, one its most prolific and renowned members worked during the twelfth century, namely, Dominicus Gundissalinus, who was also known as Gonzalo, Gonzalbo, Gonsalvi, and Gundisalvi.[2]

Not much is known about Gundissalinus's life. In fact, the dates of his birth and death are unknown. It has been suggested, however, that Gundissalinus was born in Spain either around 1100 or around 1110,[3] and it is certain that

---

[1] For a discussion of the importance for subsequent Christian thought of the translations made at Toledo, see José Luis Abellán, *Historia crítica del pensamiento español*, tomo I (Madrid: Espasa-Calpe, S.A., 1979), 210-214. On the other hand, for a discussion of the 'School of Translators of Toledo' itself, including the historical context in which it emerged as well as the texts translated there, the translators who worked there, and the method of translation used there, see Mariano Brasa Diez, O.P., "Traducciones y traductores toledanos," *Estudios filosboficos* 23 (1974): 129-137.

[2] For the variations on Gundissalinus's name, see J. García Fayós, "El colegio de traductores de Toledo y Domingo Gundisalvo," *Revista de la Biblioteca, Archivo y Museo* 33 (1932): 109-123; and Gonzalo Diaz Diaz, "Domingo Gundisalvo," in *Hombres y documentos de la filsofia española*, vol. 2 (Madrid: Consejo Superior de Investigaciones Cientificas, 1983), 590-594.

[3] The first date has been suggested by Diaz, who in "Domingo Gundisalvo," concludes: "Así pues, Domingo Gundisalvo debió nacer muy a comienzos de la doceava centuria . . ." (p. 591). The second date, on the other hand, has been suggested by Manuel Alonso Alonso, S.J., who, in his "Notas sobre los traductores toledanos Domingo Gundisalvo y Juan Hispano" in *Temas filosoficos medievales: Ibn Dawud y Gundisalvo* (Comillas: Pontificia Universitas Comillensis, 1959), 17-60, says:

he was still alive in 1190, since his name appears on a charter he signed in that year at Burgos as a member of the chapter of Segovia.[4] Moreover, it is certain that, although he was an archdeacon of the diocese of Segovia, Gundissalinus spent much of his life in Toledo, where his name appears in documents from 1178 and 1181.[5] In light of these facts, it has commonly been held that the majority of Gundissalinus's intellectual activity occurred in Toledo in the second half of the twelfth century.[6] During that period, not only did Gundissalinus translate numerous Arabic philosophical works into Latin as a leading member of the 'School of Translators of Toledo,' but Gundissalinus also wrote original philosophical works of his own.

Although, in most of his translations, Gundissalinus worked with a co-translator, Gundissalinus also seems to have translated a few works on his own, as Alonso has convincingly argued.[7] In some translations, Gundissalinus's name is associated with Ibn Daud, that is, Avendeuth.[8] In others, however, Gundissalinus's name is associated with John of Spain.[9] Though Gilson has

---

"Ignoramos la fecha de su muerte, como tampoco sabemos la de su nacimiento, que bien puede suponerse al comienzo del segundo decenio del siglo XII" (p. 25).

[4] See D. Mansilla, "La documentación pontificia del archivo de la Catedral de Burgos," *Hispania sacra* 1 (1948): 141-162; here p. 161.

[5] See C.A. González Palencia, *Los mozárabes de Toledo en los siglos XII y XIII*, tomo I (Madrid: Mestre, 1926), 141 and 154.

[6] See, for instance, H.D. Saffrey, O.P., "Gondisalvi ou Gundisalvi (Dominique)" in *Catholicisme*, tome cinquième (Paris: Letouzey et Ané, 1963), 97; and M.T. d'Alverny, "Dominic Gundisalvi (Gundissalinus)" in *The New Catholic Encyclopedia*, vol. 4 (New York: McGraw-Hill, 1967), 966.

[7] Manuel Alonso Alonso, S.J., "Las traducciones del Arcediano Domingo Gundisalvo," *Al-Andalus* 12 (1947): 295-338. For instance, on pp. 320-324, Alonso argues that Gundissalinus translated Alfarabi's *Liber excitationis ad viam felicitatis* on his own, and on pp. 333-336, Alonso argues that Gundissalinus translated Avicenna's *Liber de philosophia prima sive Scientia divina* (*Metaphysica*) on his own.

[8] This is true, for example, in the Prologue to Avicenna's *De anima*, which reads: "IOHANNI REVERENTISSIMO TOLETANAE SEDIS ARCHIEPISCOPO ET HISPANIARUM PRIMATI, Avendeuth Israelita, Philosophus, gratum debitae servitutis obsequium . . . . Quapropter iussum vestrum, Domine, de transferendo libro Avicennae Philosophi de anima, effectui mancipare curavi, ut vestro munere et meo labore, Latinis fieret certum, quod hactenus exstitit incognitum, scilicet an sit anima, et quid et qualis sit secundum essentiam et effectum, rationibus verissimis comprobatum. Habetis ergo librum, nobis praecipiente et singula verba vulgariter translatum . . ." in *Avicenna Latinus: Liber de anima seu Sextus de naturalibus*, édition critique de la traduction latine médiévale par Simone van Riet, introduction sur la doctrine psychologique d'Avicenne par G. Verbeke (Louvain: E. Peeters; Leiden: E.J. Brill, 1972), 3-4.

[9] This is true, for example, in the Explicit of Avicebron's *Fons vitae*, which reads: "Libro perscripto sit laus et gloria Christo, per quem finitur quod ad eius nomen

suggested that Avendeuth and John of Spain were different men,[10] several scholars have claimed—and in my opinion, correctly—that Avendeuth and John of Spain were actually the same man, namely, a Spanish Jew who, after converting to Christianity, was known as John of Spain.[11] Hence, either with the help of Avendeuth, that is, John of Spain, or by himself, Gundissalinus translated the following works from Arabic into Latin: (1) Hunayn ibn Ishaq's *De caelo et mundo*, which is a compilation of parts of Themistius's commentary on Aristotle's *De caelo et mundo*; (2) Alkindi's *De intellectu*; (3) the *Liber introductorius in artem logicae demonstrationis*, which is part of the *Encyclopaedia* of the Brethren of Purity; (4) Alfarabi's *De intellectu* and *Fontes quaestionum*, and perhaps his *De ortu scientiarum* and *Liber excitationis ad viam felicitatis*; (5) Alghazali's *Summa theoricae philosophiae*; (6) Avicenna's *Posteriora analytica* II, 7, *Physica* I, *Liber de philosophia prima sive Scientia divina* (*Metaphysica*), and *De anima*; and (7) Avicebron's *Fons vitae*.[12]

---

initur. Transtulit Hispanis interpres lingua Iohannis hunc ex Arabico, non absque iuuante Domingo" in *Avencebrolis* (*Ibn Gebirol*) *Fons Vitae*, ex arabico in latinvm translatvs ab Iohanne Hispano et Dominico Gvndissalino ex codicibvs Parisinis, Amploniano, Colvmbino, primvm edidit Clemens Baeumker, in *Beiträge zur Geschichte der Philosophie des Mittelalters* I, 2-4 (Münster: Aschendorff, 1892-1895), 339.

[10] Étienne Gilson, *History of Christian Philosophy in the Middle Ages* (London: Sheed and Ward, 1955): ". . . Domingo Gonzalez is usually called, in scholastic writings, Dominicus Gundissalinus. His own personality is clearly distinguishable, but some hesitation remains concerning the identities of two other translators: John of Spain (Johannes Hispanus), and Avendehut, or Avendehat, that is Ibn Daoud, or the son of David. It seems, however, that these were two distinct writers . . ." (p. 235).

[11] See, for instance, Colette Sirat, *La philosophie juive au moyen âge* (Paris: Centre National de la Recherche Scientifique, 1983), 165; Alain Guy, *Histoire de la philosophie espagnole*, deuxième édition (Toulouse: Association des Publications de l'Université de Toulouse-Le Mirail, 1985), 6-7; and Gonzalo Diaz Diaz, "Juan Hispano," in *Hombres y documentos de la filsofia española*, vol. 4 (Madrid: Consejo Superior de Investigaciones Cientificas, 1991), 532-535; see esp. pp. 532-533. That Avendeuth and John of Spain were actually the same man has been repeatedly asserted by Alonso. See his "Las fuentes literarias de Domingo Gundisalvo," *Al-Andalus* 11 (1946): 159-173; "Domingo Gundisalvo y el *De causis primis et secundis*," *Estudios eclesiásticos* 21 (1947): 367-380; "Gundisalvi y el *Tractatus de anima*," *Pensamiento* 4 (1948): 71-77; and "Notas sobre los traductores toledanos Domingo Gundisalvo y Juan Hispano," 17-60.

[12] All of the evidence concerning Gundissalinus's translations has been nicely summarized by Josep Puig in "The Transmission and Reception of Arabic Philosophy in Christian Spain (Until 1200)" in *The Introduction of Arabic Philosophy into Europe*, ed. by Charles E. Butterworth and Blake Andrée Kessel (Leiden: E.J. Brill, 1994), 7-30; see esp. pp. 12-20.

Concerning Gundissalinus's own works, on the other hand, there is some question about whether he is the author of *The Immortality of the Soul* (*De immortalitate animae*)[13] and *The Soul* (*De anima*).[14] Both of these works have often been attributed to Gundissalinus.[15] Yet, as Teske has indicated, *The Immortality of the Soul* was probably written, not by Gundissalinus, but by William of Auvergne, who was bishop of Paris from 1228 to 1249,[16] and Alonso has persuasively argued that *The Soul* was written, not by Gundissalinus, but by his co-translator, John of Spain.[17] Moreover, there is some question about whether the version of *The Sciences* (*De scientiis*) that is attributed to Gundissalinus should be numbered among his translations because it is essentially a shortened version of Alfarabi's *De scientiis*, which was later translated in its entirety by Gerard of Cremona, or whether it should be numbered among Gundissalinus's own works because it is a compilation

---

[13] The critical edition of *De immortalitate animae* was edited by Georg Bülow in *Des Dominicus Gundissalinus Schrift von der Unsterblichkeit der Seele, nebst einem Anhange, enthaltend die Abhandlung des Wilhelm von Paris "De immortalitate animae,"* in *Beiträge zur Geschichte der Philosophie des Mittelalters* II, 3 (Münster: Aschendorff, 1897).

[14] The critical edition of *De anima* was edited by J.T. Muckle in "The Treatise *De anima* of Dominicus Gundissalinus," *Mediaeval Studies* 2 (1940): 23-103.

[15] See, for instance, Maurice de Wulf, *Histoire de la philosophie médiévale*, tome deuxième, sixième édition (Louvain: Institut Supérieur de Philosophie; Paris: J. Vrin, 1936), 63; Étienne Gilson, *History of Christian Philosophy in the Middle Ages*, 237-239; Saffrey, "Gondisalvi ou Gundisalvi (Dominique)," 97; Claudia Kren, "Gundissalinus, Dominicus" in *Dictionary of Scientific Biography*, vol. 5, ed. by Charles Coulston Gillispie (New York: Charles Scribner's Sons, 1972), 592; Conrad of Prussia, *The Commentary of Conrad of Prussia on the "De unitate et uno" of Dominicus Gundissalinus*, trans. by Joseph Bobik and James A. Corbett (Lewiston, NY: The Edwin Mellen Press, 1989), 17-18; and Josep Puig, "The Transmission and Reception of Arabic Philosophy in Christian Spain (Until 1200)," 22-23.

[16] In William of Auvergne, *The Immortality of the Soul* (*De immortalitate animae*), translated from the Latin, with an Introduction and Notes, by Roland J. Teske, S.J. (Milwaukee: Marquette University Press, 1991), Teske begins his Introduction by reviewing the long-standing discussion about the authorship of *De immortalitate animae*, and he concludes by saying that "it seems safe to say that the weight of scholarly opinion and of the evidence favors the view that regards William of Auvergne as the author of *De immortalitate animae* rather than Gundissalinus" (p. 4). Also, in his "The Arabic Inheritance" in *A History of Twelfth-Century Western Philosophy*, ed. by Peter Dronke (Cambridge: Cambridge University Press, 1988), Jean Jolivet claims that *De immortalitate animae* "was most probably not by Gundissalinus at all but by William of Auvergne" (p. 143, note # 98).

[17] Alonso, "Gundisalvi y el *Tractatus de anima*." Before Alonso, Roland de Vaux, O.P., raised serious doubts about whether Gundissalinus authored *De anima* in his "La fin du *De anima* de Gundissalinus" in *Notes et textes sur l'Avicennisme latin aux confins des XIIe-XIIIe siècles* (Paris: J. Vrin, 1934), 141-146.

based, in large part, on Alfarabi's *De scientiis*.[18] Hence, there are only three works that were, without a doubt, authored by Gundissalinus: (1) *The Division of Philosophy* (*De divisione philosophiae*),[19] (2) *On Unity* (*De unitate*),[20] and (3) *The Procession of the World* (*De processione mundi*).[21]

II. The Procession of the World
A. Date of Composition

Both Baeumker and Alonso have tried to provide a date for the composition of *The Procession of the World*. Baeumker argues that, although it seems impossible to establish a chronology for Gundissalinus's works, one could "divide them with some likelihood into two groups."[22] Since Gundissalinus translated Avicebron's *Fons vitae*, Gundissalinus's references to this text may serve to distinguish his own works into two groups. There are extracts from the *Fons vitae* in *On Unity*, *The Procession of the World*, and *The Soul*, which Baeumker counts as one of Gundissalinus's works, whereas there are, Baeumker claims, either no references or dubious references to the *Fons vitae* in *The Division of Philosophy* and *The Immortality of the Soul*, which Baeumker also

---

[18] Puig maintains that *The Sciences* should be counted as one of Gundissalinus's translations; see p. 16 of his "The Transmission and Reception of Arabic Philosophy in Christian Spain (Until 1200)." Alonso, on the other hand, maintains that *The Sciences* should be counted as one of Gundissalinus's own works; see pp. 298-308 of his "Las traducciones del Arcediano Domingo Gundisalvo." Alonso edited the critical edition of *De scientiis* in *Domingo Gundisalvo: De scientiis* (Madrid-Granada, 1954).

[19] The critical edition of *De divisione philosophiae* was edited by Ludwig Baur in *Dominicus Gundissalinus: De divisione philosophiae*, in *Beiträge zur Geschichte der Philosophie des Mittelalters* IV, 2-3 (Münster: Aschendorff, 1903).

[20] The critical edition of *De unitate* was edited by Paul Correns in *Die dem Boethius fälschlich zugeschriebene Abhandlung des Dominicus Gundisalvi "De Unitate,"* in *Beiträge zur Geschichte der Philosophie des Mittelalters* I, 1 (Münster: Aschendorff, 1891).

[21] There are two critical editions of *De processione mundi*. The first was edited by Georg Bülow in *Des Dominicus Gundissalinus Schrift von dem Hervorgange der Welt* ("*De processione mundi*"), in *Beiträge zur Geschichte der Philosophie des Mittelalters* XXIV, 3 (Münster: Aschendorff, 1925). The second was established by M. Jesús Soto Bruna and C. Alonso del Real in *De processione mundi: Estudio y edición crítica del tratado de Domingo Gundisalvo* (Pamplona: Ediciones Universidad de Navarra, S.A., 1999).

[22] Clemens Baeumker, "Les écrits philosophiques de Dominicus Gundissalinus," *Revue thomiste* 5 (1897): 723-745. Discussing the chronology of Gundissalinus's works, Baeumker says: "Il paraît impossible d'établir actuellement une chronologie des œuvres de Gundissalinus. On peut cependant les diviser avec quelque probabilité en deux groupes" (p. 727).

counts as one of Gundissalinus's works. "Therefore, one seems authorized," Baeumker concludes, "to give to this last group of writings a date prior to the translation of the *Fons vitae*."[23] According to Baeumker, then, *The Procession of the World* is one of Gundissalinus's later works, along with *On Unity* and *The Soul*, because of the presence of references to the *Fons vitae* in these works, whereas *The Division of Philosophy* and *The Immortality of the Soul* are Gundissalinus's earlier works, because of the absence of references to the *Fons vitae* in these works.

Baeumker is right to conclude that *The Procession of the World* was written after Gundissalinus translated Avicebron's *Fons vitae*, because there are numerous references to this text in *The Procession of the World*. And Baeumker would most likely agree—though he does not mention this point—that *The Procession of the World* must have, in a similar way, been written after Gundissalinus translated Avicenna's *Metaphysics* and *Physics* I, because there are also numerous references to these texts in *The Procession of the World*. Yet, even if there are, as Baeumker claims, either no references or dubious references to the *Fons vitae* in *The Division of Philosophy*, it does not follow, simply from this fact alone, that this work was written before *The Procession of the World* and *On Unity*.[24] For it does not follow that, when he wrote *The Division of Philosophy*, Gundissalinus had not yet translated the *Fons vitae*: perhaps he had already translated the *Fons vitae* but did not refer to it in *The Division of Philosophy* because, given the disparate nature of the two works, the *Fons vitae* could not be a source for *The Division of Philosophy*. Hence, despite Baeumker's efforts, one cannot firmly conclude that Gundissalinus's works fall into two groups— with *The Procession of the World* in the later group—simply from a consideration of the presence or absence of references to the *Fons vitae* in Gundissalinus's works. From Baeumker's attempt to date the composition of *The Procession of the World*, therefore, it is reasonable to conclude only that *The Procession of the World* was written after Gundissalinus translated Avicebron's *Fons vitae* and Avicenna's *Metaphysics* and *Physics* I.

It is uncertain, however, precisely when Gundissalinus translated Avicebron's *Fons vitae* and Avicenna's *Metaphysics* and *Physics* I. Hence, another text must

---

[23] Ibid. Baeumker presents his argument, along with this conclusion, as follows: "On voit que Gundissalinus a traduit en latin, avec collaboration de Jean d'Espagne, *La Source de la vie* d'Avicebron. Dans les traités *De anima, De unitate, De processione mundi*, il donne incessamment des extraits de ce livre, tandis que, dans les traités *De divisione philosophiae* et *De immortalitate animae*, les emprunts faits à ce livre n'existent pas, ou sont plus que douteux. On semble donc autorisé à donner à ce dernier groupe d'écrits une date antérieure à la traduction du *Fons vitae*."

[24] I am excluding *The Immortality of the Soul* and *The Soul* from consideration, because the authorship of these works is uncertain, as I noted above, even though Baeumker attributes both of them to Gundissalinus.

be used to date the composition of *The Procession of the World*, and according to Alonso, *The Exalted Faith* (*Emunah Ramah*) of Abraham ibn Daud is such a text.[25] Alonso argues that, in *The Procession of the World*, Gundissalinus criticizes Avicebron's *Fons vitae* on several points and that Gundissalinus's criticisms are the same criticisms raised against Avicebron's *Fons vitae* in *The Exalted Faith*. Alonso infers, therefore, that Gundissalinus used *The Exalted Faith* of ibn Daud in his refutation of Avicebron in *The Procession of the World*.[26] He then notes, however, that *The Exalted Faith* was composed in either 1160 or 1168, and accepting the latter date, Alonso finally concludes that *The Procession of the World* was written sometime after 1170.[27]

Alonso's argument is convincing: it seems unreasonable to think that Gundissalinus did not use *The Exalted Faith* of ibn Daud while composing *The Procession of the World*. There is some question, however, about the date of the composition of *The Exalted Faith*, and although Alonso holds that it was written in 1168, numerous scholars have held—both before and after Alonso and, in my opinion, correctly—that it was written in 1160 or 1161.[28] In light of these considerations, then, it is reasonable to conclude that Gundissalinus wrote *The Procession of the World* no earlier than 1160, though he may have written it later.

[25] Alonso, "Las fuentes literarias de Domingo Gundisalvo."

[26] Ibid., 172. Alonso says: "De lo dicho nos parece inferirse ciertamente que, en su refutación de Ibn Gabirol, utiliza Gundisalvo la obra de Ibrahim ibn Dawud."

[27] Ibid. Alonso says: "Otra consecuencia notable es que, como el libro de Ibrahim ibn Dawud está compuesto en 1160, según Simson Weil y S. Munk, o en 1168, según Guttmann, Sarton, etc., la fecha aproximada de la composición del *De processione mundi* habrá de ser el 1170." In a footnote to this passage, Alonso refers to note # 2 on p. 159 of Simson Weil's German translation of ibn Daud's *Ha-Emunah ha-Ramah* which was published in 1852 in Frankfurt am Main. The other texts of the authors to whom Alonso refers in this passage are as follows: Solomon Munk, *Mélanges de philosophie juive et arabe*, nouvelle édition (Paris: J. Vrin, 1955), 268, which is a reprint of Munk's 1857 edition of the same work; Jacob Guttmann, *Die Religions-philosophie des Abraham ibn Daud aus Toledo* (Göttingen, 1879); Jacob Guttmann, "Abraham Ibn Daud (=David) Ha-Levi" in *The Jewish Encyclopaedia*, vol. 1 (New York: Ktav Publishing House, 1901), 101-103; and George Sarton, *Introduction to the History of Science*, vol. 2, pt. 2 (London, 1931), 368.

[28] As Alonso himself noted in the passage in the preceding footnote, both Weil and Munk argued that *The Exalted Faith* was written in 1160. This is also the view of Gershon Weiss in Abraham ibn Daud, *The Exalted Faith*, translated with commentary by Norbert M. Samuelson, translation edited by Gershon Weiss (Cranbury, NJ: Associated University Presses, 1986), 13. On the other hand, on p. 198 of *A History of Mediaeval Jewish Philosophy* (Philadelphia: The Jewish Publication Society of America, 1946), Isaac Husik has claimed that *The Exalted Faith* was written in 1161. And in at least the following three works, it is maintained that *The Exalted Faith* was written in 1160 or 1161: Abraham ibn Daud, *The Book of Tradition* (*Sefer Ha-Qabbalah*), a critical edition, with a Translation and Notes, by Gerson

B. Structure and Content

The Procession of the World consists of four parts: (1) introduction, (2) God's existence and attributes, (3) God's causality and the causality of creatures, and (4) conclusion.

1. Introduction

Gundissalinus begins *The Procession of the World* by quoting Romans 1:20: "The invisible things of God are seen, having been understood from the creation of the world by means of the things that have been made."[29] By quoting this text, Gundissalinus indicates both his goal and methodology in *The Procession of the World*.

Gundissalinus's goal is to understand the invisible things of God, that is, God's power, wisdom, and goodness. To understand these, however, the human mind must follow two paths. First, the mind must begin with sensible things and by means of resolution, that is, by analyzing sensible things into their metaphysical principles, ascend from sensible things to the contemplation of the invisible things of God. Thus, the mind begins with sensation, proceeds up through imagination, reasoning, and understanding, and finally attains intelligence. Second, after establishing God's existence and attributes, the mind must begin with God's causality and by means of composition, that is, by synthesizing the metaphysical principles of creatures, descend from the first created things to sensible things, since "the divine goodness descends to man" (p. 3) by means of created things. In *The Procession of the World*, then, Gundissalinus's goal is to understand God's power, wisdom, and goodness, and his methodology for attaining this goal will consist of an examination of created things, first, as part of his consideration of God's existence and attributes and, second, as part of his consideration of God's causality and the causality of creatures.

D. Cohen (Philadelphia: The Jewish Publication Society of America, 1967), p. XXV; Colette Sirat, *La philosophie juive au moyen âge*, 165; and Daniel Cohn-Sherbok, *Medieval Jewish Philosophy: An Introduction* (Surrey: Curzon Press, 1996), 79. Finally, an electronic search of the CD-Rom edition of *The Encyclopaedia Judaica* reveals that, in "Ibn Daud, Abraham Ben David Halevi," *The Exalted Faith* is said to have been written in 1160-1161.

[29] This text appears on p. 1 of Bülow's edition of *De processione mundi*. For all subsequent quotations, I shall indicate the page numbers from Bülow's edition in parentheses after the quotations; in the translation, these are the intralinear numbers in square brackets.

2. God's existence and attributes

Gundissalinus first presents three arguments for God's existence, and then he argues that God is uncaused, unique, and simple.

Gundissalinus's three arguments for God's existence are causal arguments that are based on an examination of sensible things. His first two arguments establish God's existence from the composition of sensible things. His third argument, by contrast, establishes God's existence from the fact that sensible things begin to be and, hence, are moved.

In his first argument, Gundissalinus claims that the sublunar world is composed entirely of heavy and light things. Heavy and light things, however, naturally move in opposite directions. Thus, there must be a cause that unites heavy and light things in the composition of the sublunar world, since these things would never come together by themselves. But this cause is God. Therefore, God exists.

In his second argument, Gundissalinus broadens his focus beyond the sublunar world, and he claims that every body, that is, every terrestrial body as well as every celestial body, is composed of matter and form. Matter and form, however, have opposite properties. Thus, there must be a cause that unites matter and form in every body in the whole world, since things with opposite properties never come together by themselves. But this cause is God. Therefore, God exists.

Hence, in each of his first two arguments for God's existence, Gundissalinus establishes that God exists as the conserving cause of the composition of sensible things. From these early passages of *The Procession of the World*, then, it is evident that Gundissalinus rejects deism, that is, the view that, although God initially caused the universe, God now neither conserves nor causally interacts with creatures. Instead, as will become clear from his discussion of God's causality and the causality of creatures, Gundissalinus endorses concurrentism, that is, the view that God not only initially created the universe from nothing (*ex nihilo*) but also now conserves creatures and causally interacts with them by way of primary and secondary causality.

In his third argument for God's existence, which is based largely on principles ultimately found in Aristotle's *Physics* III, 1 and VII, 1, Gundissalinus claims that some sensible things begin to be. For some sensible things are corrupted, and only things that begin to be are corrupted. But a thing that begins to be goes forth from potency to act, and the going forth from potency to act is motion. So, a thing that begins to be is moved. But everything that is moved is moved by another. Thus, a thing that begins to be had its being caused by something else. For something cannot be the efficient cause of itself, since something cannot move itself, nor can the being of a thing that begins to be be caused by what does not exist, since a non-existent thing cannot move anything. That other thing, however, either began to be or did not begin to be. If it too began to be, then some third thing caused its being. Hence, either (1) we will proceed to infinity so that there will be an infinite series of beings in which each member of the series began to be and was, consequently, brought into being by a previous member of the series or (2) there exists a being that did not begin to be but that caused the being of each thing that began to be. Gundissalinus assumes, however, that we cannot proceed to infinity. Accordingly, there must exist a being that did not begin to be but that caused the being of each thing that began to be, and this being, Gundissalinus contends, is eternal. For whatever did not begin to be is eternal. But God is this eternal being, who is, in this way, "the principle and first cause of all things" (p. 5). Therefore, God exists.[30]

With God's existence established, Gundissalinus considers God's attributes. After claiming that God is eternal, which he did in his third argument for God's existence, Gundissalinus argues that God is uncaused, unique, and simple. To establish these conclusions, Gundissalinus uses a cluster of arguments from Avicenna's *Metaphysics* I, 6 and 7.

God is uncaused, Gundissalinus argues, because everything that exists is either a possible being or a necessary being. God is not, however, a possible being. For a possible being has its being only in relation to its cause. Thus, if God were a possible being, God, who is the first cause of all things, would have a cause and would not, consequently, be the first cause of all things, which is impossible. Hence, God is a necessary being. But a necessary being is uncaused. For a necessary being is necessary through itself, not in relation to a cause. Thus, if God were caused, God would exist only in relation to his cause, and as a result, God would be both necessary through himself and not necessary through himself, which is impossible. Therefore, because he is a necessary being, God is uncaused.

God is, moreover, unique: there is one and only one God. Gundissalinus establishes this conclusion with two lengthy series of arguments: in the first, he argues that there cannot be two necessary beings that exist together and accompany each other in the necessity of being (*necessitas essendi*); and in the second, he argues—principally by contending that the necessity of being must be instantiated in only one being—that there must be only one necessary being.

Finally, God is simple, Gundissalinus argues, because every possible being is composite. For, when it is considered in itself, a possible being is always

---

[30] For a more detailed analysis of Gundissalinus's three arguments for God's existence, see pp. 49-63 of Bruna's Introduction and Commentary in *De processione mundi: Estudio y edición crítica del tratado de Domingo Gundisalvo*.

possible, but when it is considered in relation to its cause, a possible being is necessary through another thing. Thus, every possible being is composite because "what it has, when it is considered in itself, is one thing, and what it has from another thing is something else" (p. 16). Therefore, because he is a necessary being and not a possible being, God is not composite but is, instead, simple.

In his consideration of God's existence and attributes, then, Gundissalinus argues in a systematic fashion: first, by examining sensible things, he concludes that God exists as the eternal, first cause of all things; then, since God is the first cause of all things, Gundissalinus concludes that God is a necessary being, not a possible being; finally, since God is a necessary being, he concludes that God is uncaused, unique, and simple. Hence, much like Aquinas's arguments in the *Summa theologiae* and *Summa contra Gentiles*, Gundissalinus's arguments successively build on one another until each point is established. In this part of *The Procession of the World*—and, indeed, throughout the entire work—Gundissalinus's argumentation is highly systematic.

3. God's causality and the causality of creatures

There are five parts to Gundissalinus's discussion of God's causality and the causality of creatures: (1) a brief description of God as the primary cause and creatures as secondary causes; (2) a brief overview of the three types of causality exercised by God and creatures, namely, creation, composition, and generation; (3) a detailed analysis of God's causality and, in particular, creation; (4) a brief sketch of the constitution and division of creatures; and (5) a brief explanation of the causality of creatures.

According to Gundissalinus, God is the primary cause. As such, God is "the first and efficient cause of all things" (p. 17) and is also "the cause of moving for all other things" (p. 17). In himself, however, God is unmoved, as Gundissalinus shows from the fact that God is the first principle and is, consequently, sufficient and complete. Thus, although God, as the primary cause, causes all creatures and their motions, God's essence is unmoved.

Creatures, on the other hand, are secondary causes, and in the most general way, a secondary cause may be described, according to Gundissalinus, as "that by which something is bestowed upon third and fourth causes, and so on, from which and in which something is produced, such as celestial spirits, soul, nature, and many other things—all of which are effects of the first cause—and it is the cause of the things that follow" (p. 19). Thus, although they are caused and moved by God, creatures, as secondary causes, are causes of other creatures, as Gundissalinus will explain in greater detail below.

As the primary cause and as secondary causes, God and creatures exercise three types of causality: creation, composition, and generation. God acts by creation and primary composition. In creation, God produces the first simple principles of creatures out of nothing, and these principles, as Gundissalinus will later argue, are matter and form. In primary composition, on the other hand, God unites the first simple principles of creatures. As Gundissalinus will later contend, however, God acts neither in time nor in space. Hence, God's act of creating matter and form is prior to God's act of uniting matter and form by nature and causality, but not in order, time, or place.

Creatures, on the other hand, act by secondary composition and generation. In secondary composition, creatures unite things composed of matter and form, which have already been united by God in primary composition. In generation, however, creatures produce things that begin and perish, and unlike creation and primary composition, generation, which follows secondary composition, occurs in time.

After presenting this brief overview of creation, composition, and generation, Gundissalinus offers a detailed analysis of God's causality and, in particular, creation. In systematic fashion, Gundissalinus first discusses the object of creation, that is, matter and form, and then he discusses the nature of God's creative act. In both instances, Gundissalinus draws liberally upon Avicebron's *Fons vitae*.

The object of creation is matter and form, the first simple principles of things. There needed to be two created principles instead of one, Gundissalinus argues, because what God created needed to differ from him. Thus, since God is one, what God created could not have been one but needed to be two. Moreover, the two principles God created needed to differ from each other, because constitution can come about only from different things. Thus, in order that a universe of creatures might be constituted from them, the two principles God created needed to differ from each other. Hence, they could not have been two pieces of matter or two forms. Therefore, "one necessarily had to be matter and the other form" (p. 21).

Matter and form, however, exist in two ways: in potency and in act. Matter by itself exists in potency, and form by itself exists in potency. In other words, the potential being of matter and the potential being of form is the being each of them has by itself separately from the other. Matter and form exist in act, however, when they are united. Thus, before they are united, matter and form each have being in potency, but when they are united, matter and form are both brought forth from potency to act.

Since actual being is produced when matter and form are united, Gundissalinus argues that matter does not exist in act before form and that form does not exist in act before matter. Likewise, matter does not exist in potency before form, nor does form exist in potency before matter. Nonetheless, when matter and form are united, form gives being to matter, while matter receives form.

For, Gundissalinus argues, matter always remains after any type of change, but form comes and goes. Yet, when form comes, it constitutes a thing, and when form goes, a thing is destroyed. Hence, matter receives form, and by coming to matter, form gives being to matter.

In act, therefore, matter exists under the determination of form, and form exists with matter. But where does matter exist in potency? Gundissalinus replies that "matter, when it is understood by itself without form, has being in potency, namely, that being which it has in the wisdom of the creator" (p. 27). In potency, therefore, matter exists in God's wisdom, and the same is true of form.

It is clear, then, what relation exists between matter and form, on the one hand, and being, on the other: matter and form have being in potency and being in act. Yet, what should be said about unity or oneness and substantiality? How are these metaphysical categories related to matter and form?

Gundissalinus claims that whatever has being has being because it is one. Given this metaphysical principle, two conclusions follow. First, since form gives being to matter so that matter and form may both exist in act, it follows that oneness is form. For, like form, oneness is the cause of actual being. Second, since being is proportional to oneness and since matter and form have being in act when they are united, oneness and being in act emerge together when matter and form are united. Thus, although oneness is form, oneness and the being in act of matter and form are simultaneous by nature.

Substantiality, on the other hand, may be considered in two ways. For "substance" may be applied either to matter insofar as it exists in potency separately from form or to matter insofar as it exists in act as having already received form. In the proper sense, however, "substance" is applied to matter considered insofar as it exists in act as having already received form. Thus, the same is true of substantiality as is true of oneness: substantiality emerges when matter and form are united. In other words, substantiality emerges together with the being in act of matter and form. Therefore, concerning the relation between substantiality and oneness, on the one hand, and matter and form, on the other, Gundissalinus concludes: "it must not be said that substantiality and oneness are forms of matter and form as if they were different from them, but they are matter and form" (pp. 30-31). Substantiality and oneness are, consequently, simultaneous with the being in act of matter and form.

Matter and form first acquired being in act, however, in two stages: first, they were created by God from nothing (*ex nihilo*); then, they were united to each other by God in primary composition. God created matter and form from nothing outside of himself, that is, from nothing of a subject (*ex nihilo subjecti*), because, before matter and form were created, God alone existed. Thus, there was nothing besides God from which matter and form might have been created. On the other hand, God created matter and form from nothing of himself (*ex nihilo sui*). For, given that God alone existed before matter and form were created, matter and form could have been created only from God or not from God, that is, from nothing of God. Drawing upon the *De essentiis* of Hermann of Carinthia,[31] Gundissalinus makes a distinction between creation and making, on the one hand, and generation and procession, on the other, and he says that what is from God (*de ipso*) is "nothing other than him, but is the same as he is and, therefore, was neither made nor created, but was generated or proceeds" (p. 35). Thus, since they are other than God, matter and form were not generated from God, nor do they proceed from God; they were, instead, created not from God, that is, from nothing of God. Nonetheless, because neither matter nor form can exist in act without the other, God first created matter and form and then united them to each other in primary composition. Yet, as Gundissalinus notes, since God does not act in time, the creation of matter and form preceded their composition with each other only by causality, not in time. It was in two stages, then, that matter and form first acquired being in act: first, they were created by God from nothing of himself and of a subject (*ex nihilo sui et subjecti*); then—with respect to causality, not in time—they were united to each other by God in primary composition.

With this conclusion established, Gundissalinus considers the view of one of the "theologians" (p. 36), namely, Hugh of St. Victor, who claims that first matter was a mixture of the four elements in which the earthy element was positioned in the center and was enveloped by an opaque cloud composed of a blending of water, air, and fire.[32] According to Hugh, God first created matter as a mixture—or chaos—of the four elements, and then he distinguished the four elements by means of form in order to produce corporeal creatures. Hence, on this view, which Hugh offers as an interpretation of the account of creation given in Genesis, matter existed in act independently of form, which was subsequently united with matter in act so that corporeal creation might be produced.

After first indicating that this view is false because it is contrary to the teachings of the philosophers, Gundissalinus gives two arguments to show that first matter could not have been a mixture—or chaos—of the four elements.

---

[31] The critical edition of Hermann's *De essentiis* is found in *Hermann of Carinthia: De essentiis*, a critical edition, with Translation and Commentary, by Charles Burnett (Leiden: E.J. Brill, 1982).

[32] In "Hugo de San Victor refutado por Domingo Gundisalvo hacia el 1170," *Estudios eclesiásticos* 21 (1947): 209-216, Alonso has shown that Hugh of St. Victor is the theologian Gundissalinus has in mind in this portion of *The Procession of the World*. By comparing a passage from Hugh's *The Sacraments of the Christian Faith* with this portion of *The Procession of the World*, Alonso has indicated that the two texts are almost identical.

First, the elements are composed of matter and form. Thus, since whatever is composed of something else is posterior to the things of which it is composed, the elements are posterior to matter and form. Hence, first matter could not have been a mixture of the four elements because, if it were, it would have been posterior to matter and form, which are prior to the elements, and consequently, first matter would not have been first, which is absurd. Second, whatever is broken down into other things, Gundissalinus says, comes after the things into which it is broken down. Thus, since first matter—viewed as a mixture of the four elements—is broken down into the four elements, which are, in turn, ultimately broken down into matter and form, first matter— viewed as a mixture of the four elements—comes after matter and form. Hence, first matter could not have been a mixture of the four elements because, if it were, first matter would not have been first, which is absurd. As Gundissalinus showed above, therefore, both matter and form were first created by God, and then—with respect to causality, not in time—they were united to each other by God in primary composition.

Gundissalinus uses two images to explain the nature of God's creative act. In the first image, Gundissalinus likens God's creation of things, which is "only the going forth of form from his wisdom and will and the impression of his image in matter" (p. 40), to the flowing of water emanating from its origin. In the second image, Gundissalinus likens God's creation of things, which results in "the sealing of form in matter" (p. 41), to a mirror receiving the shape of one who is looking into it: "matter receives form from the divine will, just as a mirror receives a shape from one who is looking into it" (p. 41). Concerning the nature of God's creative act, then, Gundissalinus disagrees with Avicenna, who holds that things emanated necessarily from the essence of God, the necessary being, whereas Gundissalinus agrees with Avicebron, who holds that things came from God freely through the divine will, not necessarily by emanating from the divine essence.

Having discussed God's causality and, in particular, creation, Gundissalinus presents a brief sketch of the constitution and division of creatures. With respect to the constitution of creatures, Gundissalinus maintains both the doctrine of universal hylomorphism, which asserts that everything except God is composed of matter and form, and the doctrine of a plurality of forms in creatures. He argues that substantiality was the first form united with matter and that, since everything that has being has being because it is one, unity accompanied substantiality when it was first united with matter by God. Thus, substantiality and unity are the first of all forms. Once, however, matter has received substantiality and unity, it is further distinguished by subsequent forms, namely, corporeity and spirituality, and by virtue of these forms, the whole of matter is completely divided into two kinds of substance, namely, corporeal and incorporeal substance. According to Gundissalinus, then, everything except God is composed of matter and form, and there is a plurality of forms in creatures, whether they are corporeal creatures or incorporeal, that is, spiritual, creatures. Hence, to use one of his own examples, a stone is composed of matter and form, and in the stone, there is one form by virtue of which the stone is a substance, another by virtue of which the stone is one, a third form, namely, the form of corporeity (*forma corporeitatis*), by virtue of which the stone is a corporeal substance as opposed to an incorporeal substance, and so on. Both the doctrine of universal hylomorphism and the doctrine of a plurality of forms in creatures, which were to appear repeatedly in the Franciscan tradition in the thirteenth and fourteenth centuries, have been attributed to Avicebron,[33] from whom Gundissalinus most likely borrowed them, though the doctrine of a plurality of forms in creatures seems ultimately based on the Porphyrian tree.[34]

With respect to the division of creatures, Gundissalinus notes that what is composed of matter and form was, at first, divided into corporeal and incorporeal substance. Corporeal substance is, in turn, distinguished into (1) the four elements, (2) bodies composed of the four elements, that is, terrestrial or sublunar bodies, and (3) bodies that are neither the four elements nor composed of the four elements, that is, the celestial bodies. Incorporeal substance, on the other hand, is distinguished into (1) the rational substances, which are the angels, the spirits of the planets, human souls, and demons, and (2) the irrational substances, which are the sensitive soul, the vegetative soul, and nature. Only terrestrial or sublunar bodies and the irrational incorporeal substances are corruptible. All other creatures, because they were produced from the first union of matter and form, which are simple things, are incorruptible. Hence, in all of reality, there are three types of beings: (1) God, who alone is eternal and who, consequently, has neither a beginning nor an end; (2) perpetual creatures, which are incorruptible and which, consequently, have no end though they have a beginning; and (3) generated creatures, which are corruptible and which, consequently, have both a beginning and an end.

With the constitution and division of creatures clarified, Gundissalinus offers a brief explanation of the causality of creatures. In this explanation, as I noted earlier, Gundissalinus rejects deism and endorses concurrentism, and

---

[33] See, for instance, Fernand Brunner, *Platonisme et Aristotélisme: La critique d'Ibn Gabirol par Saint Thomas d'Aquin* (Louvain: Universitaires de Louvain, 1965).

[34] As Bülow astutely observes in note # 2 on pp. 47-48 of his edition of *De processione mundi*, Gundissalinus seems to presuppose the Porphyrian tree when he argues that there is a plurality of forms in creatures. For the logical classification system known as the Porphyrian tree, see pp. 35-36 of Porphyry's *Isagoge*, trans. by Edward W. Warren (Toronto: The Pontifical Institute of Mediaeval Studies, 1975).

in doing so, he bases his view, at least in part, on the *De essentiis* of Hermann of Carinthia.

Gundissalinus first distinguishes between God, as the primary cause, and creatures, as secondary causes. He says:

> [S]ince an artisan uses an instrument in acting, certainly there was also an artisan and an instrument in creation and composition. But in generation, mixing, change, and other sorts of composition, which are of second or third rank, the artisan adapted to himself another instrument, that is, a secondary cause, so that indeed he made the first things by himself, namely, by creating matter and form from nothing and by combining them with each other, but he entrusted the second and, in order, the third and fourth things to his servant, a secondary cause, to be carried out by its governance and undertaking. Hence, in the beginning there was a twofold cause, namely, a primary and a secondary cause. The primary cause is God; the secondary is his instrument drawn from his very works (p. 51).

God is the primary cause. As such, God acts as an artisan in his act of creation and primary composition. God does not, however, use an extrinsic instrument in his act of causality. Rather, by himself, God creates matter and form from nothing and unites them with each other in primary composition to cause the incorporeal substances, including the angels and nature, the celestial bodies, and the four elements. For, as Gundissalinus earlier noted, "from the first union of matter and form, only three kinds of things are seen to have proceeded, namely, the invisible creature, celestial bodies, and the four elements" (p. 48).

The incorporeal substances, including the angels and nature, the celestial bodies, and the four elements are, consequently, God's proper effects as the primary cause. At the same time, however, these creatures are God's instruments with respect to other creatures, and as such, they are secondary causes that act as God's servants. Thus, Gundissalinus continues:

> [T]he secondary cause is itself a product of the first composition, and all the motions after creation and composition, which are the motions of the first cause, serve it and follow its authority, but at the command of the first cause. Therefore, of secondary causes, which are the instrument of the first cause, the first is the angelic creature, the second is the motion of the heavens, the third is nature, and then the rational soul and some others (p. 51).

Hence, although creatures, as secondary causes, act as servants at God's command, they are causes in their own right, because all the motions after God's act of creation and primary composition arise from the authority of creatures. Moreover, as causes in their own right, creatures—in particular, angels, the celestial bodies, and nature—operate in three worlds: (1) in the first world, which is beyond the firmament and is incorporeal and incorruptible, angels move the celestial souls, that is, the spirits of the planets; (2) in the second world, which stretches from the firmament all the way to the moon and is corporeal and incorruptible, the celestial bodies move the lower bodies that are contiguous with and contained within themselves, including all sublunar bodies; and (3) in the third world, which is below the moon and is corporeal and corruptible, nature acts by means of the four elements to cause generated things.

God's operation, by contrast, is not restricted to any particular sphere of reality. "Its own world," Gundissalinus insists,

> is not assigned to the first cause, because it presides everywhere and rules every-where. It is neither enclosed by a place, nor is it bounded by time. And all other causes do nothing except at its command (p. 53).

As the primary cause, then, God is omnipresent and acts neither in space nor in time. Yet, with secondary causes, which act at God's command, "places are assigned to some, times to some, and both places and times to still others" (p. 53).

Since God is omnipresent as the primary cause, Gundissalinus concludes that God moves all things. But God moves all things, Gundissalinus adds, "in a different way" (p. 54). Through himself and without any means, God moves the intelligences, that is, the angels. By means of other things, however, God moves everything else. "Therefore," Gundissalinus concludes,

> in the first world the first secondary cause [i.e., an angel] receives from the first cause a command concerning all these things that it subsequently brings about in what is lower. In the second world, on the other hand, the second secondary cause [i.e., a celestial body] receives motion from the first secondary cause in order to move whatever lower thing it touches. In this third world, the third secondary cause [i.e., nature] operates by various motions insofar as it is com-manded by the causes that preside over it (pp. 53-54; brackets added).

4. Conclusion

Gundissalinus concludes *The Procession of the World* by summarizing the progression of the universe as it was brought into being in act from nothing by God, and borrowing from Avicebron's *Fons vitae*, he likens the constitution of the universe to the order of numbers.

The progression of the universe from nothing to being in act required that "first of all, the first simple things should be made from nothing by creation, and that from the simple things composed things should be made by the first union of the simple things, and then that from the composed things the things composed of the elements should be made by generation" (p. 54). Thus, as

Gundissalinus argued above, matter and form were created by God from nothing of himself and of a subject (*ex nihilo sui et subjecti*); they were then united to each other by God in primary composition; finally, from creatures composed of matter and form, generated things that are composed of the four elements were made. "And in this way," Gundissalinus says, "a progression was made from nothing to simple things, from simple things to composed things, and from composed things to generated things" (p. 54).

The universe finally constituted in act in this way may be likened to the order of numbers. For, as Gundissalinus notes, "the most wise creator willed to establish all things according to the order of numbers" (p. 55). Hence, corresponding to the numbers one, two, three, and four, there are four beings: (1) God, who is the first true and simple unity; (2) matter and form, which are the two simple unities that are the metaphysical principles of all created beings; (3) perpetual beings, such as the rational incorporeal substances, that are composed of matter and form alone are, like the number three, indivisible and are, consequently, incorruptible; and (4) generated beings that are composed of the four elements and are, consequently, corruptible. "And every creature," Gundissalinus concludes, "exists according to these well-ordered arrangements" (p. 56).

C. Sources and Significance

Gundissalinus uses three types of sources in *The Procession of the World*: scriptural, poetic, and philosophical. In ten passages, he explicitly quotes or alludes to texts from Scripture, including both the Old and New Testament. This indicates that *The Procession of the World* is the work of a philosopher who is, at the same time, a Christian. On the other hand, Gundissalinus quotes a text from Ovid's *Metamorphoses* while discussing the creation of first matter. More than any other type of source, however, Gundissalinus draws upon philosophical works.

On one occasion, Gundissalinus refers to Augustine and Apuleius by name. Gundissalinus borrows this passage, however, from Book II of the *De essentiis* of Hermann of Carinthia, who himself refers to Augustine and Apuleius by name: Hermann cites Augustine's *The City of God* and Apuleius's *The God of Socrates*. Gundissalinus also refers to Plato by name on one occasion and to Aristotle by name on another occasion, though, in each case, he may be referring to the work of someone else: when he mentions Plato, he may be referring to Apuleius's *Plato and his Doctrine*; when he mentions Aristotle, he may be referring to ibn Ishaq's *On the Heavens and Earth*. In most passages, however, Gundissalinus does not give references by name; rather, he uses phrases such as "it is said that" (p. 2) or "the philosophers say that" (p. 51). In some cases, these vague references make it extremely difficult to determine his sources with certainty. In other cases, however, his sources are clear. Thus, near the beginning of *The Procession of the World*, he refers to texts from Boethius's *The Trinity* and *The Consolation of Philosophy*, and as I indicated above, he refers, as Alonso has shown, to Hugh of St. Victor's *The Sacraments of the Christian Faith* on one occasion and to *The Exalted Faith* of Abraham ibn Daud on several occasions. More than those of anyone else, however, Gundissalinus uses texts from Hermann of Carinthia, Avicenna, and Avicebron. Though he never refers to Hermann, Avicenna, or Avicebron by name, Hermann's *De essentiis*, Avicenna's *Metaphysics* and *Physics* I, and Avicebron's *Fons vitae* are certainly Gundissalinus's principal sources in *The Procession of the World*.

As Baeumker has correctly noted, the greater part of *The Procession of the World* is a compilation.[35] For instance, Gundissalinus's discussion of God's attributes has been borrowed from Avicenna's *Metaphysics* I, 6 and 7, and his discussion of creation and the constitution of creatures has been borrowed from various portions of Avicebron's *Fons vitae*. Indeed, in the entirety of *The Procession of the World*, there are no fewer than twenty-two passages that correspond to Hermann of Carinthia's *De essentiis* and no fewer than fifty-seven passages that correspond to Avicebron's *Fons vitae*. *The Procession of the World* is a significant work, nonetheless, for at least two reasons.

First of all, in *The Procession of the World*, Gundissalinus is the first in the Latin West to articulate some of the basic metaphysical doctrines of Christianity in light of the Platonism, Aristotelianism, and Neoplatonism of Muslim and Jewish Arabic philosophy.[36] Principally in light of Avicenna's *Metaphysics* and Avicebron's *Fons vitae*, Gundissalinus argues that God exists, that God is unmoved, uncaused, unique, and simple, that God has wisdom and a will, and

---

[35] Baeumker, "Les écrits philosophiques de Dominicus Gundissalinus." Referring to *The Procession of the World*, Baeumker says: "Ce livre est habilement composé. La plus grande partie néanmoins est une compilation" (p. 741).

[36] This point has been repeatedly noted. Thus, in the Introduction and Commentary in *De processione mundi: Estudio y edición crítica del tratado de Domingo Gundisalvo*, Bruna says: "El *De processione mundi* . . . [r]epresenta en efecto el pensamiento original de Gundisalvo, más allá de su labor como traductor y transmisor a Occidente de una parte considerable de la filosofiá árabe; pensamiento original en la medida en que pertenece ya a la madurez de su labor intelectual y tiene—como venimos diciendo—la intención de exponer las tesis fundamentales de la cosmo-visión cristiana en relación con las nuevas ideas transmitidas a través del descubrimiento de los textos árabes" (p. 21). In "Gundisalvi (Dominique), Gundissalinus, Gondisalvi" in *Dictionnaire d'histoire et de géographie ecclésiastique*, vol. 22 (Paris: Letouzey et Ané, 1988), R. Aubert claims that "[l]e rôle de Dominique Gundissalvi a surtout consisté à introduire dans le monde des écoles occidentales le mélange de philosophie néoplatonicienne et aristotélicienne élaboré dans le monde arabe" (p. 1169). Finally, in his *Historia crítica del pensamiento español*, Abellán notes that "Gundisalvo fue el primer pensador occidental que sufrió la influencia de las obras

that God freely created the world from nothing of himself and of a subject (*ex nihilo sui et subjecti*).[37] This is an attempt—the same attempt that would be so common in the thirteenth century among the Scholastics—to affect a reconciliation between Christianity and ancient Greek philosophy as it was transmitted and transformed by Muslim and Jewish Arabic philosophers, such as Avicenna and Avicebron.

Second, in his attempt to establish some of the basic metaphysical doctrines of Christianity, Gundissalinus always remains focused on the organization of *The Procession of the World*, and for each issue he considers, as I indicated above in connection with his discussion of God's existence and attributes, Gundissalinus argues systematically. It is clear that the organization of *The Procession of the World* was at the forefront of Gundissalinus's mind while he was writing the work because, when he borrows arguments from Avicenna and Avicebron, Gundissalinus frequently changes the order of those arguments from their original texts, texts which he himself had translated. For instance, while discussing God's attributes, Gundissalinus rearranges the sequence of Avicenna's arguments from *Metaphysics* I, 6, and while discussing creation, he does the same with arguments from Avicebron's *Fons vitae*. Indeed, throughout *The Procession of the World*, Gundissalinus selects arguments from all five books of the *Fons vitae*, but the sequence in which he uses those arguments almost never corresponds to the sequence in which they appear in the *Fons vitae*. And the same is true for the *De essentiis* of Hermann of Carinthia. This shows that, according to Gundissalinus, good organization requires that certain philosophical issues be considered before others, and the attempt to achieve good organization permeates *The Procession of the World*.[38] Thus, after stating his goal and methodology at the beginning of *The Procession of the World*, Gundissalinus first establishes God's existence from a consideration of sensible

---

árabes y fue agente decisivo en la incorporación de las mismas al mundo latino" (p. 215).

[37] In this sense, there is truth in the assertion of M.T. d'Alverny, who says: "Gundisalvi was not an original thinker, but it would be unfair to qualify him as a mere compiler. He tried earnestly to adapt the teachings of Avicenna and Avicebron to the use of Latin Christians in the West" on p. 966 of "Dominic Gundisalvi (Gundissalinus)."

[38] Given this, Jolivet's observation concerning Gundissalinus's works cannot be accepted. In "The Arabic Inheritance," Jolivet says: "Gundissalinus works chiefly with scissors and paste; he has not yet reached the stage of integrating the new philosophical contribution into compositions with an organization of their own" (p. 134). Part of the significance of Gundissalinus's *The Procession of the World* is found precisely in the fact that, in this work, Gundissalinus is concerned with good organization. And this is not surprising, when one considers Gundissalinus's other works. For instance, as Henri Hugonnard-Roche has shown in "La classifi-

things; then he discusses God's attributes and explains God's creation of the world; finally, he considers the constitution and division of creatures, including God's causal interaction with creatures by way of primary and secondary causality. This organization, that is, an organization wherein one considers— in order—God's existence, God's nature, the procession of creatures from God, the constitution of the created world, and the ontological relation between God and creatures, is the same organization that would so clearly characterize the *Summae* of the thirteenth century, as is evident, for instance, from Aquinas's *Summa theologiae* and *Summa contra Gentiles*.[39] For these two reasons, .then, Gundissalinus is, as M. de Wulf has noted, one of "the forerunners of the systematic thinkers."[40] Therefore, despite the fact that Gundissalinus borrows a good deal from Avicenna and Avicebron as well as Hermann of Carinthia, *The Procession of the World* is a significant work because it is a true precursor to Scholasticism.[41]

---

cation des sciences de Gundissalinus et l'influence d'Avicenne" in *Études sur Avicenne*, dirigées par Jean Jolivet et Roshdi Rashed (Paris: Société d'Édition Les Belles Lettres, 1984), Gundissalinus's *The Division of Philosophy* is rigorously structured and craftily organized: "Le *De divisione philosophie* de Gundissalinus est sans aucun doute le produit d'une large compilation de sources très nombreuses et d'origines très diverses, hellénistique, latine et arabe . . . . Mais loin d'être une simple juxtaposition de citations ou de paraphrases, le traité de Gundissalinus est, comme nous croyons l'avoir souligné, une classification fortement structurée et subtilement organisée" (pp. 59-60). The same type of organization is present in *The Procession of the World*.

[39] In this sense, there is truth in Saffrey's assertion, in "Gondisalvi ou Gundisalvi (Dominique)," that Gundissalinus "marque le point de départ d'un genre de spéculation philosophique et d'argumentation théologique qui porta ses fruits au XIII siècle" (p. 97).

[40] M. de Wulf, *Histoire de la philosophie médiévale*: "précurseurs des esprits systématiques" (p. 62).

[41] The way in which *The Procession of the World* influenced particular Scholastic thinkers is, of course, another question. Broaching this issue in his *History of Christian Philosophy in the Middle Ages*, Gilson says the following about *The Procession of the World*: "Despite its many borrowings from Avicenna and Gabirol, this treatise is of very good philosophical quality and its influence may have been wider than we suppose. Thomas Aquinas seems to have both read and reinterpreted its proofs of the existence of God by the Prime Mover, by efficient causality, [and] by possibility and necessity" in note # 3 on p. 653. In "Gondisalvi ou Gundisalvi (Dominique)," this observation is also offered by Saffrey, who notes that *The Procession of the World* "contient des preuves de l'existence de Dieu, qui semblent avoir été lues et réinterprétées par S. Thomas d'Aquin" (p. 97). In presenting his proofs for God's existence, however, Aquinas explicitly cites neither Gundissalinus nor his *De processione mundi*. Hence, in the absence of another reason to affirm it, it must

III. The Latin text of *The Procession of the World* and the Translation and Notes

As I noted above, there are two critical editions of *De processione mundi*: Bülow's 1925 edition and a 1999 edition established by Bruna and Alonso del Real. Bülow's edition has been the basis of my translation because, although it is more recent, the text of Bruna and Alonso del Real's edition differs from the text of Bülow's edition in only two respects: (1) in Bruna and Alonso del Real's edition, each paragraph is numbered, which is not the case in Bülow's edition; and (2) the punctuation of Bruna and Alonso del Real's edition differs slightly from that of Bülow's edition. These differences seemed so minor to me that I concluded that there was nothing to be gained by translating Bruna and Alonso del Real's edition instead of Bülow's edition, though the lexicon of Latin terms provided on pp. 237-262 of Bruna and Alonso del Real's edition is a welcomed, considerable improvement on Bülow's edition that should be extremely helpful to those wishing to use the Latin text of *The Procession of the World*.

In the translation, I included the page numbers from Bülow's edition in square brackets. In several passages, I modified the paragraph breaks of Bülow's edition because, in each case, the sense of Gundissalinus's argument seemed to require either that the current paragraph should continue or that a new paragraph should be started. In a few passages, I added words that are not in the Latin in order to produce a smoother translation; these words appear in square brackets. Also, whenever I was unsure about the translation of a word or phrase, I included the Latin in parentheses immediately following my translation. In only four cases did I suggest an alternate reading of the text in Bülow's edition, and in each case, I noted what Bülow's edition reads and why I thought an alternate reading was required. Finally, in one case, I did not translate Bülow's reconstruction of a sentence that is corrupted in all of the manuscripts; instead—and I noted this—I translated the sentence as it appears in Burnett's edition of the *De essentiis* of Hermann of Carinthia, because Gundissalinus borrows the passage in question from Hermann.

In the notes to the translation, I relied upon Bülow's citations of sources, though I also added a good number of additional citations not noted by Bülow, especially for Hermann of Carinthia's *De essentiis*, which Bülow never cites,

---

remain a conjecture that Aquinas was influenced in his proofs for God's existence by Gundissalinus's *The Procession of the World*.

and for Avicebron's *Fons vitae*. In notes containing citations to relatively short passages that have not already been translated into English, I translated the passages in the hope that this would be helpful to readers. Finally, when I thought Gundissalinus's arguments became a little too dense, I added explanatory notes.

I want to note, in conclusion, that I was helped with this project from beginning to end by Rev. Roland J. Teske, S.J. When I first considered translating Gundissalinus's *De processione mundi*, Fr. Teske encouraged me to do so; as I completed different sections of the translation, he carefully reviewed them, making needed corrections and offering wise suggestions for improvement; finally, when I wrote the Introduction, Fr. Teske read it closely and—as is his habit—in a timely fashion, pointing out several respects in which I could improve it. In these ways, not only did Fr. Teske help me complete this project—something for which I thank him—but he also gave me yet another example of an ideal that he repeatedly exemplified when he was my teacher and that I was taught years ago by other good Jesuits like him, namely, to be a man for others.

THE PROCESSION OF THE WORLD
(*De processione mundi*)

By

Dominicus Gundissalinus

The invisible things of God are seen, having been understood from the creation of the world by means of the things that have been made.[1] For, if we vigilantly observe these visible things, we will ascend by means of these same things to the contemplation of the invisible things of God. After all, the wonderful works of this visible creation are traces of the creator, and for this reason we come to him by following through these works, which are from him. Hence, in the Book of Wisdom it is written: "Through the greatness and beauty of creation, the creator can be seen by means of the intellect."[2] For, since greatness, beauty, and usefulness are set forth to be admired so much, the power, wisdom, and goodness of the creator, which are the invisible things of God, are certainly revealed. After all, he would not make such great things unless he were powerful, nor such beautiful things unless he were wise, nor such useful things unless he were good. Hence, it is written about Wisdom: "In the ways she reveals [2] herself cheerfully, and in every thought she meets them."[3] For the ways to the creator are his works. Provided we observe them diligently, we attain knowledge of his hidden things in some way or another.

Hence, to understand the invisible things of God, a threefold matter of investigation is proposed for us: namely, in the composition and disposition of things and the efficient (*mouente*) cause of each of them. Composition is the principle from which some union is brought about. Disposition is the ordered relation of the united elements. But one efficient (*mouens*) cause is primary, another secondary, another is of the third rank, and so forth.[4]

---

[1] Romans 1:20.
[2] Book of Wisdom 13:5.
[3] Book of Wisdom 6:17.
[4] In Book II of his *De essentiis*, Hermann of Carinthia says: "The matter of all speculation is divided into three: the composition of things, the disposition of things,

For this investigation, however, three things are necessary: namely, reasoning, demonstration, and intelligence. For reasoning deals with composition; demonstration with disposition, and intelligence with the cause.[5] Hence, it is said that it is necessary to conduct oneself with natural things in a rational way (*rationaliter*), with mathematical things in an instructive way (*disciplinaliter*), and with theological things in an intelligent way (*intelligentialiter*).[6] And indeed, possibility is sufficient for reasoning; necessity is sufficient for demonstration, but a certain simple and mere conception is sufficient for intelligence.[7] However, we rise to intelligence through understanding or through demonstration, to understanding through reasoning, to reasoning through the imagination, and to the imagination through sensation. For sensation apprehends sensible forms along with matter that is present; [3] imagination apprehends sensible forms along with matter that is not present; reasoning apprehends sensible forms apart from matter; the intellect apprehends intelligible forms only. But in a similar way intelligence somehow apprehends one simple form.[8] By these degrees, therefore, the human mind ascends to the contemplation of God, and the divine goodness descends to man. Reason investigates by composing and resolving. By resolving, it ascends; by composing, it descends. For, in resolution, it begins from the last things; in composition, it begins from the first things. Hence, the creature of the world sees the invisible things of God that have been understood by means of the things that were made, since reason deals with composition in this way.

This whole world, which the sphere of the moon encircles, consists entirely of heavy and light things. But the motion of heavy things is to go downwards, and the motion of light things is to go upwards. Since, therefore, heavy and light things have it from their nature to go in opposite directions, they would

---

and the cause governing both. The composition is the mixture of the constituent causes. The disposition is the ordered arrangement of the mixed causes . . . . The governing cause is divided into three: a principal cause, a secondary cause, and a cause of third degree of worth" on p. 181 of *Hermann of Carinthia: De essentiis*, a critical edition, with Translation and Commentary, by Charles Burnett (Leiden: E.J. Brill, 1982). Burnett's edition contains both the Latin text of Hermann's *De essentiis* and, on the facing pages, Burnett's translation. In references to Hermann's *De essentiis*, I shall either use Burnett's translation, as I have in this note, or simply cite the book, page(s), and line number(s) of Hermann's Latin text in Burnett's edition.

[5] Hermann of Carinthia, *De essentiis* II: "Reason is applied to the composition, demonstration to the disposition, and intellect to the governing cause" (p. 181).

[6] Boethius, *The Trinity*, ch. 2.

[7] Hermann of Carinthia, *De essentiis* II, p. 180, ll. 16-17.

[8] This distinction among sensation, imagination, reasoning, and the intellect—each of which has its own object—is made by Boethius in *The Consolation of Philosophy* V, 4.

by no means come together in the composition of this corruptible world unless some compelling cause were joining them together. The sublunar world, therefore, is composed by something else.

Likewise, every body consists of matter and form.[9] For every body is a substance and has some quantity and quality. But form and matter have opposite properties. For one sustains, and the other is sustained;[10] one [4] receives, and the other is received;[11] one forms, and the other is formed.[12] Things, however, that have opposite properties never by themselves come together in order to constitute something. Form and matter, therefore, do not come together by themselves in the constitution of a body. When, however,

---

[9] In Book II, Chapter 2 of his *Metaphysics*, Avicenna says: "It is now evident, therefore, that bodies are composed of matter and form." The Latin text of this passage, which I have translated for this note, is in vol. 1, p. 82, ll. 43-44 of *Avicenna Latinus: Liber de Philosophia Prima sive Scientia Divina*, édition critique de la traduction latine médiévale par Simone van Riet, introduction doctrinale par G. Verbeke (Louvain: E. Peeters; Leiden: E.J. Brill, 1977, 1980, 1983). References to this work will be as follows: Avicenna, *Metaphysics*, with the book, chapter(s), page(s), and line number(s) in Van Riet's edition. In all cases, the translation is mine. According to Avicebron, however, everything except God is composed of matter and form, and hence, every body is composed of matter and form. Thus, in Book IV, Chapter 6 of his *Fons vitae*, Avicebron says: ". . . all things are composed of matter and form. This is because body, which is positioned at the lower extreme, is composed of matter and form, namely, because it is a substance having three dimensions. And if the whole of things that exists is continuous and extended from the higher extreme all the way to the lowest extreme and the lowest extreme is composed of matter and form, it is established, consequently, that everything that exists from the beginning of the higher extreme all the way to the lowest extreme is also composed of matter and form." The Latin text of this passage, which I have translated for this note, is on pp. 225-226, ll. 23-7 of *Avencebrolis (Ibn Gebirol) Fons Vitae*, ex arabico in latinvm translatvs ab Iohanne Hispano et Dominico Gvndissalino ex codicibvs Parisinis, Amploniano, Colvmbino, primvm edidit Clemens Baeumker, in *Beiträge zur Geschichte der Philosophie des Mittelalters* I, 2-4 (Münster: Aschendorff, 1892-1895). References to this work will be as follows: Avicebron, *Fons vitae*, with the book, chapter(s), page(s), and line number(s) in Baeumker's edition. In all cases, the translation is mine.

[10] Avicebron, *Fons vitae* V, 23, p. 299, l. 16: "Matter sustains, and form is sustained . . . ."

[11] According to Avicebron, matter receives, and form is received. Thus, he says the following about matter in *Fons vitae* V, 42, p. 335, ll. 9-11: "Form comes from above, and matter receives it from below because matter is a subject by the fact that it has being under form; and form is sustained upon it." And he says the following about form in *Fons vitae* III, 55, p. 202, ll. 1-2: ". . . the reception of form in matter from an efficient power comes about only in accordance with the preparation of matter for this . . . ."

[12] According to Avicebron, form forms, and matter is formed. Thus, in *Fons vitae* V, 28, p. 307, l. 27, he says that ". . . matter was formed by form . . . ."

things that do not come together by themselves—in fact, when things opposed to each other—are found in something, they clearly reveal that they have a cause that put them together. Therefore, every body has a cause that put it together.[13] In this way, therefore, the whole world has such a cause.

Moreover, everything that exists either begins to be or does not begin to be; either it has a beginning or it is without a beginning. However, the breaking down of this sensible world clearly indicates that some things have a beginning. For we see that many things here cease to be which would never cease unless they had at some time begun. For nothing perishes that does not begin, and a breaking down of parts comes only after a putting together.[14] For whatever the understanding distinguishes and breaks down into something was composed from these things into which it is broken down.[15] Since, therefore, we see that many things composed of so diverse components are continually being corrupted and broken down and yet since nothing is corrupted except what was generated—but everything that is generated begins to be made because it was not—it is certainly necessary that we say that whatever we see is corrupted began at some time.

Something, however, gave being to everything that begins to be. And before everything that begins to be exists, it is possible that it be, because what cannot

---

[13] In this portion of his argument, Gundissalinus uses principles that are also maintained by Avicebron, namely, that matter and form have different essences—and are, in fact, opposed to each other—and that they consequently must be united to each other by something else. Thus, in *Fons vitae* V, 2, p. 260, ll. 12-16, Avicebron says: "D: In what does matter differ from form, when the essence of each of them is considered? M: Each of them differs from the other through itself. And I do not mean here a difference of things in agreement, but I mean a difference of opposition and true contrariety . . . ." Given the difference and, indeed, opposition between their essences, matter and form must, according to Avicebron, be united to each other by the power of God, the powerful one. So, in *Fons vitae* V, 32, p. 316, ll. 3-6, he says: "D: Since everything is united only to something like and agreeing with it, how is it possible that matter and form are united, since there is not a likeness between them? M: It is this that shows, in a greater way, the power of the powerful one." Hence, as Avicebron concludes in *Fons vitae* V, 33, p. 318, ll. 12-14, matter and form ". . . are bound by [God's] will and obedient to it because, although they are different in essence, nonetheless they are united simultaneously."

[14] Gundissalinus's assertion is an almost verbatim reproduction of an assertion made by Hermann of Carinthia. In Bülow's edition, Gundissalinus's text reads: "Nihil enim occidit, quod non oritur, nec solutio nisi compositionem sequitur" on p. 4, ll. 12-13. In Burnett's edition of Hermann's *De essentiis*, Hermann's text reads: "Nec enim occidit nisi quod oritur; nec solutio, nisi compositionem sequitur" on p. 84, ll. 1-2.

[15] Avicebron, *Fons vitae* II, 16, p. 51, ll. 17-19: "Whatever part of composed things the understanding distinguishes and breaks down into something else is composed from that into which it is broken down . . . ."

be never begins to be, but what can be begins to be. Likewise, when it begins to be, it goes forth from potency to act, from possibility to act. The going forth, however, from potency to act is motion.[16] Therefore, whatever begins to be is moved towards being. Everything, however, that is moved is moved by another.[17] Everything, therefore, that began [5] to be did not give being to itself, but some other thing gave being to it. For, when it was not, it could not give being to itself. After all, what is not cannot give being either to itself or to another thing. It is also impossible that something be the efficient cause of itself. For every efficient cause is prior to what it causes. If, therefore, something were to give being to itself, then it would be before and after itself, which is impossible. For this reason, some other thing gave being to everything that begins to be.

That other thing, likewise, either began to be or did not begin to be. But, if it begins to be, then something else gave being to it. And by investigating in this way, either we proceed to infinity or we will come to something that gave being to the things that begin to be, but it by no means began to be.[18] What exists, however, and did not begin to be is eternal. Therefore, it—whatever it is—is before all the things that have a beginning, and in this way it is the principle and first cause of all things.

But the first cause does not have a cause. Otherwise, it would no longer be the first. This is proved as follows. Everything that exists either is a possible being or is a necessary being. But some cause is the first. Therefore, the first cause either is a possible being or is a necessary being. However, everything that is a possible being, when it is considered in itself, has both its being and its non-being from a cause. When it exists, it has already received being as distinguished from non-being, but when it does not exist, it already has non-being

---

[16] Aristotle, of course, defines motion as the act of what is in potency precisely insofar as it is in potency in *Physics* III, 1. Avicebron, however, uses this general definition of motion in his analysis of motion in place, that is, locomotion. Thus, in *Fons vitae* III, 6, p. 90, ll. 4-5, Avicebron says that "[e]verything that is moved by means of local motion is continually proceeding from potency to act."

[17] The ultimate source of this proposition seems to be Aristotle's *Physics* VII, 1. Gundissalinus does not argue for the truth of this proposition, unlike later medieval philosophers who had access to Aristotle's works. For instance, in *Summa contra Gentiles* I, 13, Aquinas argues that it is true that everything that is moved is moved by another by presenting a succinct and clear explanation of the three arguments Aristotle uses in the *Physics* to establish this proposition. Gundissalinus, on the other hand, simply takes this proposition as true.

[18] Gundissalinus now assumes, however, that there cannot be an infinite series of beings in which each member of the series begins to be and was, consequently, brought into being by a previous member of the series. Hence, the other disjunct is true: there must exist something that gave being to the things that begin to be while it itself in no way began to be.

as distinguished from being. And it must be that either it has each of those two from something else or [6] it does not have each of them from something else. If it has them from something else, it will certainly exist from a cause. But it is impossible that it does not have them from something else. For it is evident that nothing can come into being except by something else that has being. The same is true with respect to non-being. After all, either a thing is sufficient by itself to have being, or it is not sufficient. If, however, it is sufficient by itself to receive both, then, when it has being, it will be a being through itself, and it will be a necessary being. It was assumed, however, that it is not a necessary being. Therefore, it is simultaneously necessary and possible, which is contradictory. If, however, it is not sufficient for itself to have being through itself, but there is something else from which its being comes—and yet, for everything whose being is from the being of something other than itself, that which brought all things into being is certainly its cause—then something previously possible has a cause, and it will not have through itself any of those two factors that were received except through a cause. For, the concept of being is taken from that which is the cause of being, and the concept of non-being is taken from a cause that deprives a thing of being. We say, therefore, concerning the meaning of possible being that the being that it has it has from and in relation to its cause. For, although it has being only when its cause exists, it is, nonetheless, a possible being, though it has being or non-being and it is not bound to either [7] of those two. It has been shown, therefore, that whatever is a possible being has being only in relation to its cause.[19] The first cause, therefore, is not a possible being. It is, therefore, a necessary being. Hence, it does not have a cause.

For it is evident that a necessary being does not have a cause. For, if a necessary being had a cause of its being, its being would certainly be through that cause. However, the being of everything whose being is through something else would, when it is considered in itself, not be necessary. And yet the being of whatever, when considered in itself without something else, is not found to have necessary being will not be necessary through itself. Hence, it is established that, if a being necessary through itself has a cause, it is not a being necessary through itself. It is evident, therefore, that a necessary being does not have a cause.

Indeed, it is also clear, from this, that it is impossible for one thing to have necessary being through itself and to have necessary being through something else. For, if the necessity of its being is through something else, then it is

---

[19] This argument to show that the first cause does not have a cause because it is not a possible being that exists only in relation to a cause but is, instead, a necessary being closely parallels Avicenna's argument in *Metaphysics* I, 6, pp. 44-46, ll. 38-71.

impossible for it to exist without the other thing. It is impossible, therefore, [8] that it have necessary being through itself. For, if it is a necessary being through itself, that other thing certainly does not contribute anything in regard to its being. For everything to which something else contributes in regard to being is not a necessary being through itself. Therefore, a necessary being does not have a cause.[20]

We also say that it is not possible that what is a necessary being have another necessary being so that this one exists together with that one and that one with this one and so that one of them is not the equal cause of the other but so that they accompany each other as equals in the necessity of being. For, when each of them is considered by itself without the other, either it will be necessary through itself or it will not be necessary through itself. If, however, it is necessary through itself, either it will have necessity also with the other, when it is considered with the other—and if this is so, then it will be necessary through itself and necessary through something else, and this is absurd, as we showed above—or it will not have necessity along with the other so that its being follows upon the being of the other and accompanies it. Its being will, on the contrary, not depend on the being of the other so that this one exists only if that one exists, and vice versa.

If, however, it is not necessary through itself, it is necessary that, when it is considered by itself, it be a possible being but that, when it is considered along with the other, it be a necessary being. And then it must be that that other being either is the same way or is not the same way. If, however, that other thing is the same way, then it must be that the necessity of being of this being comes from that being, although that being is either a possible being or a necessary being. If, however, the necessity of being of this being comes from that being, then that being is a necessary being. But it does not have necessary being through itself nor through some other third being, as we said before, but through that being, which, in turn, has the necessity [9] of being from it. And the necessity of being of this being brings with it the necessity of being of that being, which, on the contrary, had being after the necessity of being of this being—and this by means of an essential posteriority. Accordingly, this being will never have necessary being through itself in any way. If, however, the necessity of being of this being comes from that being though that being is a possible being, then the necessity of being of this being will come from that being, which exists as possible and does not give to this being the necessity of being and does not receive from it the possibility of being, but the necessity of being. Therefore, the possibility of being of that being will be the cause of the

[20] These two arguments to show that the first cause does not have a cause because it is a necessary being are almost verbatim reproductions of Avicenna's arguments in *Metaphysics* I, 6, p. 44, ll. 24-37.

necessity of being of this being, and this being will not be the cause of the possibility of being of that being. Therefore, they will not accompany each other [as necessary beings], since each of them is by itself the cause and by itself the effect.

Then also it happens that, since the possibility of being of that being is the cause of the necessity of being of this being, then the being of this one does not proceed from its being, but from the being of that being. We supposed, however, that they accompanied each other.

Therefore, they cannot accompany each other in being, unless perhaps both depend on another extrinsic cause. And it will then be necessary either that one of them is by itself first or that there is some other extrinsic thing that gives them being in terms of the relation of being that they have between themselves and establishes the relation between them in terms of which they have being. One of a pair of relative beings, however, does not give being to the other, but it exists simultaneously with it, but the being of [two] given [relative] things is the cause that unites them. Even two pieces of matter or two substances alone are not sufficient by themselves to give to themselves the being that is said of them, but they need some other third thing, which [10] unites them with each other. For it is necessary that one of two alternatives be the case, namely, either that the being and certitude of each of these things exists only when it exists with the other or that it will not be necessary that each exists along with the other. [If the first alternative is true,] then, in this way, its being will not, therefore, be necessary through itself. Therefore, it will be possible and, consequently, caused. Hence, it and its cause, as we said, will not accompany each other in being. Its cause, therefore, will be some other thing. Therefore, this being and that being will not be the cause of the relation that exists between them, but that other thing will be. [If, however, the second alternative is true,] then for this being to exist together with that one will, of course, be an accident useless for its proper being. Hence, its proper being will not come from the concomitance of the thing that accompanies it insofar as it accompanies it, but from a preceding cause, if it is caused. Therefore, in that case either its being will be from its companion (*ex comitante*), not insofar as it is its companion (*comitans*), but from the being proper to [its] companion (*comitanti*)—and in this way, they will not be companions (*comitantia*), but cause and effect, and its companion (*comes*) will also be the supposed cause of the supposed relation that exists between them, as in the case of a father and a son—or they will be companions (*comitantia*) insofar as neither of them is the cause of the other, and the relation [between them] will be necessary for their being. But the first proper cause of the relation [between them] will be an extrinsic cause establishing their two essences, as you knew, and the relation [between them] will be an accident. Hence, it will not have a companionship except through a separable or an inseparable accident. This is other than the case in question; however, what exists through an accident will indubitably exist from a cause. Hence, from the side of the companionship there will be two effects. And thus, neither of them is a necessary being by itself.[21]

We will also say that the necessary being must be one [11] in itself. But if there were many and each of them would be a necessary being, it is necessary that each of them either does not differ or does differ from the other in its essence in some way. If, however, one does not differ from the other in the concept of its proper essence, but one differs from the other insofar as the one is not the other—for this is without doubt a difference—one certainly differs from another through something that is apart from the concept of its essence. For in these necessary beings the concept of the essence is not different. But something is added to it by which it is made this being, or something exists in this being by which it is made this being. And yet, in that necessary being, it is not united to something. Something, however, is added to each of the others by which this being is made this being, and conversely, because this thing is this thing, the same thing is the other. For these beings are the same in essence, and [yet] there is otherness in them; there is [some] other diversity. In this way, therefore, let us hold that each of them is the same in essence with the other and differs from the other.

Therefore, I say that the things that are attached to the essence from the outside are to be regarded as consequent, not essential accidents. If, however, these consequent accidents come to the essence from the fact that it is the essence, then it is necessary that all necessary beings agree in terms of them. We already said, however, that they differ in terms of them. They, therefore, agree and differ in [12] the same things, which is absurd. Or if diversity comes to them from intrinsic causes, not from causes added to their essence, then, if that cause did not exist, they certainly would not differ. Therefore, if that cause did not exist, their essences would be one. But their essences are not one. Therefore, if that cause did not exist, each of them would not have necessary being through itself separate from the other. The necessity of being, therefore, of each of them is proper and singular from an intrinsic cause. We already showed, however, that whatever is a being necessary through something else is not a being necessary through itself.[22] On the contrary, possible being is found in the definition of its essence, since, just as each of these is a necessary being through itself, so each is also a possible being through itself, which is absurd.

---

[21] This series of arguments to show that there cannot be two necessary beings that exist together and accompany each other in the necessity of being closely parallels Avicenna's arguments in *Metaphysics* I, 6, pp. 46-48, ll. 72-38.

[22] In this case, the something else through which these beings are necessary is the intrinsic cause of their necessity, as opposed to an extrinsic cause of their necessity.

Let us suppose, however, that they differ in some essential accident, since they agree in the concept of their essence. But this accident in which they differ is impossible unless it is either necessary or not necessary to the necessity of being for each of them. If, however, it is necessary to the necessity of being, it is then necessary that everything that is a necessary being agree in it. If, however, it is not necessary for the being of the necessity of being, then the necessity of being is separate from it and is necessity through itself. That essential accident is, however, added from the outside and comes to their necessity after the fullness [13] or perfection of the necessity of their being. We already showed, however, that this is absurd. Therefore, these necessary beings must differ in no way.

We must, however, show this yet again in another way. For it is impossible for the necessity of being to be divided into many except in one of two ways, namely, either as things are divided by differences or as they are divided by accidents. We know, however, that differences are not included in the definition of what is set down as a genus. Therefore, they do not give a genus its essence, but they give it being in act, as is the case, for example, with "rational." For "rational" does not add anything to the genus "animal" with regard to animality, but it adds to it so that it may be a determinate essence (*essentia appropriata*) in act. Therefore, it is necessary that the differences of the necessity of being, if there perhaps are any, add something with regard to the essence of the necessity of being only for its being in act. This, however, comes about in two ways. In one way, the proper essence of the necessity of being is only the ceaselessness of being (*incessabilitas essendi*), not like the essence of animality, which is an essence apart from the essence of the ceaselessness of being, for being is something that follows upon it or that is added to it, as you knew. Therefore, differences do not add anything to the necessity of being except for that which is within the essence of its form. We already ruled this out in another way, and in order that this necessity of being might have being in act, it is necessary that it depend on another thing that gives it. Hence, the meaning [14] of necessity by which a thing is a necessary being will depend on something else. We were speaking, however, about a being necessary through itself. Therefore, the thing will be a necessary being through itself and a necessary being through something else, a possibility that we already excluded. It is evident, therefore, that the necessity of being is not divided throughout them as a genus is divided by differences.

It is also evident that the essence to which the necessity of being belongs cannot be something generic, which is divided by differences or by accidents. It remains, therefore, that it be something specific. We say, however, that it is impossible that the necessity of being be something specific that is predicated of many things. For, since the individuals of any species, as we already showed, are not diverse in terms of the concept of their essence, they must be diverse because of their accidents. We already showed, however, that no accident can be present in the necessity of being.

We are also able to show this same point briefly in another way. For we say that, when the necessity of being is said of something in which it is, either it is wholly proper to it, because it has being only by it and not apart from it nor the being of another thing—and in this way, it is necessary that the necessity of being be had only by one individual thing—or this thing has it either possibly or necessarily. Hence, this thing will not be a necessary being through itself, although it is a necessary being through itself, which is impossible. Therefore, only one thing alone can have the necessity of being. [15]

If, however, someone says that, although this one thing has the necessity of being, another thing is not, nonetheless, prevented from having it, or that, although another thing has it, this thing is not, nonetheless, prevented from having it, we say that we are speaking of the necessity of being only insofar as it is proper to this thing, insofar as it belongs to this thing without consideration of some other thing. For it is impossible that this same property belong to another thing, but only another property similar to it and of the same form, which is due to it, just as that property is due to this thing.

We also state in another way that if, by reason of the fact that each of them is a necessary being, each is itself, then whatever is a necessary being is itself and not something else. But if by reason of the fact that it is necessary being, it is not itself but necessary being is added to that which is to be itself, it certainly has this union either from itself or from something else. But if it has it from itself and if it is itself by reason of the fact that it is necessary being, then whatever is necessary being is itself. But if it has it [16] from something else, then it has it from a cause that is other than it. The fact, therefore, that it is itself comes from a cause, and the property of being, which is proper to it alone, comes from a cause. It, therefore, is something caused. But it is necessary that it be one without any companion. For it is not like a species under a genus and like one under number; it is not like individuals under a species, but the concept of that name has only it itself. Hence, something else does not share with it in its being. We will, however, explain this elsewhere.[23]

These are the properties that necessary being has. We have, however, already displayed the property of that which is possible being. For its property is that it does not lack something else by which it might have being in act. But everything that is a possible being, when it is considered through itself, is always a possible being. At times, however, it happens that it is necessary through another thing. And what exists in that way either does not have the necessity

---

[23] This series of arguments to show that there is only one necessary being closely parallels Avicenna's arguments in *Metaphysics* I, 7, pp. 49-54, ll. 40-42.

of being always but only at certain times—and what exists in that way must have matter, which precedes it in time, as we will soon show—or it has the necessity of being always and through another thing—and what exists in that way is not entirely simple. For what it has, when it is considered in itself, is one thing, and what it has from another thing is something else. For it has the fact that it exists from both, namely, from itself and from something else. And on this account, nothing is so first and so simple that it does not have some possibility and potency in itself except necessary being alone.[24]

It is established, therefore, that necessary being is neither relative nor mutable nor many but single, since no other thing participates in its being, which is proper to it.[25] And this is none other than God alone, who is the first cause and first principle of all things, [17] which is necessarily understood to be one only, not two or more. For the one is prior to two.[26] For, everything that, when eliminated, eliminates another thing and, when present, makes the other thing present is prior to that other thing. But unless one comes first there will not be two. Or, if there are two, it is necessary that there be one. But this is not reversible so that, if there is one, there are two or there must be two. Therefore, there cannot be two principles. Each of them is said to be working to be first. But neither of them abandons the first position to the other. For, unless one were prior to the other, there would by no means be a first [principle] of all things.[27] Therefore, there is one principle, there is one efficient cause, of all things.

As was said before, however, one cause is primary, another secondary, and another the last. The primary cause is an efficient cause, since it moves by its own power in order that something may be developed. And this is the first and simple cause, which, although it is unmoved, is the cause of moving for all other things. Hence, it is called stable because, while remaining, it makes all things be moved. For every motion begins from rest, and for this reason it is necessary that what is unmoved should precede, by its antiquity, everything that is moved. Therefore, it is necessary that the unmoved that moves all things be the

---

[24] This argument to show that the necessary being alone is truly simple closely parallels Avicenna's argument in *Metaphysics* I, 7, pp. 54-55, ll. 42-55.

[25] Gundissalinus's concluding statement about the nature of the necessary being is an almost verbatim reproduction of Avicenna's assertion in *Metaphysics* I, 6, p. 43, ll. 22-23 that ". . . the necessary being is not relative or mutable or many, nor does something else share with it in its being, which is proper to it."

[26] Hermann of Carinthia, *De essentiis* I: "For one is prior to two . . ." (p. 79).

[27] Hermann of Carinthia, *De essentiis* I: "Moreover, when there are two, there must also be one, but the opposite—that if there is one, there will be two—does not hold true. How, then, can two principles even be considered, when, since each of them is struggling to be prior, the principal place is left to neither? For unless one of the two is prior to the other, in no way could one be the principle of all things . . ." (p. 79).

first and efficient cause of all things.[28] And this cause of the universe is God the creator.

Hence, that whose potency is always in act cannot be moved because there is nothing by which or to which it may be moved. For, as was said before, motion is the going forth from potency to act. Therefore, only what is imperfect is moved. It is moved, however, so that it may be perfected [18] by that to which it is moved. If, therefore, the first principle is moved, then it would be imperfect. But it is clearly demonstrated that prior to everything imperfect there is something perfect in comparison with which it is called imperfect. For every imperfection is a privation of perfection. If, therefore, the first principle were moved, then it would be moved by something else. For this reason, some other thing would be seen to be prior to it in comparison with which it would seem imperfect.

Moreover, everything that is moved is moved by something else. But everything by which something is moved is the efficient cause of the motion of the thing that is moved. Every efficient cause, however, is prior to that whose cause it is. Therefore, everything by which something is moved is prior to the thing that is moved. If, therefore, the first principle were moved, then it would be moved by something else that would be prior to it. In this way, therefore, the first principle would not be first.

Moreover, whatever is moved is moved to something, since whatever is moved is moved from potency to act. In fact, potency and act are opposites. But whatever is moved to something does not have that to which it is moved.[29] For, if it already had it, it would not be moved to it, but it would rest in it. For the end of motion is the attainment of that on account of which and to which the whole motion takes place. If, therefore, the first principle were moved, something would certainly be lacking to it, to acquire which it would be moved. And thus, it would be insufficient. Hence, it is necessary that some other thing be sufficient and complete through which it would be perfected. And that same thing either would be moved or would not. If, however, it were moved, then the same conclusion that was brought about from the preceding reasoning would follow and so on to infinity.[30] It remains, therefore, that

---

[28] Gundissalinus borrows this consideration of God's stability, that is, God's immutability, and God's antiquity from Hermann of Carinthia, *De essentiis* I, pp. 78 and 80, ll. 25-4.

[29] Avicebron, *Fons vitae* V, 10, p. 275, l. 25: ". . . whatever is moved to something lacks that thing . . . ."

[30] That is, there would be an infinite series of beings in which each member of the series would be insufficient and incomplete and, thus, would need to be perfected by a previous member of the series. Gundissalinus assumes, however, that such a series is impossible.

something be the first principle, which is moved in no way; and this is what is called God.[31]

Hence, every motion is foreign to his essence. For all [19] of his motion is in his works, just as the power in an author is always the same in composing and resolving.[32] In a subject, however, composition is one thing, resolution another; nor are these motions found together in the same thing.

A secondary cause, however, is that by which something is bestowed upon third and fourth causes, and so on, from which and in which something is produced,[33] such as celestial spirits, soul, nature, and many other things—all of which are effects of the first cause—and it is the cause of the things that follow, about which we will speak later. The last cause, however, is the end of every intention[34] so that, just as the first cause is that which nothing else precedes, the last cause is that which anything else precedes.[35] In between these, there are many intermediate causes, each of which is the effect of what precedes it and the cause of what follows after it.

And because nothing that the first cause moves is produced by a cause without motion, the motion of the causes, therefore, must be distinguished. Therefore, one of the motions of the first cause, by which the first cause moves, is called creation, whereas the other is called composition.[36] But creation is

[31] Gundissalinus's way of referring to God here calls to mind Aquinas's way of referring to God at the end of each of the five ways in *Summa theologiae* I, q. 2, a. 3.

[32] In his edition of *De processione mundi*, Bülow notes that, in all of the manuscripts, the text for this sentence is corrupted to such an extent that he could not correct it and amend it precisely: "Textus huius loci (pag. 18, 12 Omnis—19, 2 resoluens) in omnibus codicibus corruptissimus est, ita, ut eum prorsus sanare et emendare non possim" in note # 1 on p. 18. His reconstruction of the sentence is this: "Omnis uero motus est in opere eius, quemadmodum uirtus in auctore quidem semper eas componens et resoluens" on pp. 18-19, ll. 27-2. Yet, this passage of *The Procession of the World*—including the material before and after this sentence—is borrowed from the *De essentiis* of Hermann of Carinthia, and in Burnett's edition, Hermann's text for this sentence reads as follows: ". . . omnis namque motus eius, in opere eius. Quemadmodum virtus quidem in auctore semper eadem, et componens et resolvens . . ." on p. 86, ll. 5-7. Instead of translating Bülow's reconstruction of this sentence, I have translated the sentence as it appears in Hermann's text.

[33] Hermann of Carinthia, *De essentiis* II: "But the secondary cause is that through which something is administered. Third and fourth (and further) causes are those out of which, and in which, something is made" (p. 155).

[34] Hermann of Carinthia, *De essentiis* II: "The ultimate cause is the destination of every aim" (p. 155).

[35] I am reading *alia nulla* as *alia ulla*, since this is required by the sense of the passage. Gundissalinus's point is that, just as there is nothing else before the first cause, so there is nothing else after the last cause, not nothing else before the last cause. Hence, anything else—not nothing else—precedes the last cause.

[36] Hermann of Carinthia, *De essentiis* I: "Of all the movements of the primordial cause there are two general categories—creation and generation . . ." (p. 87). Thus,

first; composition is second. However, the motion of some secondary causes is composition only, whereas the motion of others is generation. For one type of composition is primary, whereas the other is secondary. Primary composition arises from simple things. Secondary composition arises from composed things, and one type of secondary composition is natural, whereas the other is artificial. And creation, of course, arises from the very first of the first principles out of nothing.[37] Composition, however, is the arising from those principles of the first things that, once they have been made, never perish, inasmuch as they were put together as a result of the first formation. Generation, however, arises from the same principles, and it is the renewal, not of the things [20] that were composed, but of the things that continuously begin and perish, as if from remaining small things a drawing out of things has, once again, been produced. Creation and composition, however, are seen to be related to each other such that, although creation is seen to be prior by nature and causality, it should, nonetheless, never be understood as prior in order, time, or place. Since generation, however, comes down by means of composition, it necessarily comes later in time.[38]

But since nothing begins to be without motion, for this reason all things that have a beginning have a beginning either by creation or by composition or by generation. Hence, all things that truly and properly have a beginning either were created from nothing or were made out of some things by composition or from some things by generation or at times by the corruption of another form, although in the Scriptures some seem to be used for others, but not in the proper sense.

By creation, therefore, the first principles of things, which were created from nothing, have a beginning. These are the material principle and the formal principle. For the creator created some principle. But every created thing must be different from the creator.[39] Since, therefore, the creator is truly one, something created certainly ought not to have been one. But just as there was

---

both Gundissalinus and Hermann attribute two motions to God: they both attribute creation (*creatio*) to God; but, whereas Hermann attributes generation (*generatio*) to God, Gundissalinus attributes composition (*compositio*) to God.

[37] Hermann of Carinthia, *De essentiis* I: "Creation is of principles, at the beginning, out of nothing" (p. 87).

[38] Hermann of Carinthia, *De essentiis* I, p. 110, ll. 15-23. In this text, Hermann distinguishes generation (*generatio*) into two types, namely, primary and secondary. Gundissalinus, on the other hand, distinguishes composition (*compositio*) into two types, namely, primary and secondary, and then, unlike Hermann, he considers generation (*generatio*) as a third, distinct type of causality that is subsequent to creation and composition.

[39] Avicebron, *Fons vitae* IV, 6, p. 222, ll. 25-26: ". . . the creator of all things must be one alone, and the created thing must be different from him."

nothing in the middle between the creator and the first creature,[40] so there is nothing in the middle between one and two.[41] For the first thing that is different from one is two. Since, therefore, the creator is truly one, the creature that is after him certainly had to be two.[42] For diversity is not found in oneness, but in otherness. But the first principle of otherness is twoness, which first departs from oneness. If, therefore, the first created thing were one, then there would be no diversity.[43] But, if there were no diversity [21], there would be no universe of creatures that was going to be. Therefore, two simple principles, from which all things were to be constituted, had to be created first by one simple principle.

Constitution, however, can come about only from different things. For this reason, the two simple principles had to be different. But they could not be two pieces of matter. For from two or more pieces of matter without form nothing can be constituted. For, since all being comes from form,[44] if both were matter,

[40] By claiming that there is nothing in the middle between the creator and the first creature, Gundissalinus disagrees with the opinion of Avicebron. For, according to Avicebron, God's will is in the middle between God's essence and the first created thing. In *Fons vitae* I, 7, pp. 9-10, ll. 28-4, Avicebron says: "M: . . . in being there are only these three: namely, matter and form, the first essence, and the will which is in the middle of the extremes. D: What is the reason that there are only these three in being? M: The reason for this is this, that, with respect to every created thing, there must be a cause and something in the middle between them. The cause, however, is the first essence; the created thing [is] matter and form; [and] the will is in the middle of them." There is, nonetheless, some question about the exact sense in which, according to Avicebron, God's will is in the middle between God's essence and the first created thing and about the precise metaphysical relation that exists between God's will and God's essence. For a discussion of this issue, see my "Weisheipl's Interpretation of Avicebron's Doctrine of the Divine Will: Is Avicebron a Voluntarist?" which is forthcoming in the *American Catholic Philosophical Quarterly*.

[41] Avicebron, *Fons vitae* V, 31, p. 315, l. 10: ". . . between one and two there is nothing in the middle . . . ."

[42] Avicebron, *Fons vitae* V, 12, p. 279, ll. 3-4: ". . . since the creator of things is one, it is necessary that the created thing be two."

[43] Avicebron, *Fons vitae* V, 23, p. 300, ll. 16-17: ". . . if the created thing were one, there would be no difference here because difference arises only below the One."

[44] This metaphysical principle, namely, that all being comes from form (*ex forma sit omne esse*), also appears in Gundissalinus's *De unitate*: "For all being comes from form, that is to say, in created things." The Latin text of this passage, which I have translated for this note, is on p. 3, ll. 10-11 of *Die dem Boethius fälschlich zugeschriebene Abhandlung des Dominicus Gundisalvi "De Unitate,"* Herausgegeben und Philosophiegeschichtlich behandelt von Paul Correns, in *Beiträge zur Geschichte der Philosophie des Mittelalters* I, 1 (Münster: Aschendorff, 1891). References to this work will be to page(s) and line number(s), and in all cases, the translation is mine. This principle is also found, however, in numerous texts in Avicebron's *Fons vitae*; see, for instance, *Fons vitae* III, 39, p. 168, l. 24; IV, 5, p. 221, l. 12; V, 8, p.

then there would be no being. Similarly, neither could they be two forms. For form cannot subsist without matter.[45] Therefore, both could not be matter, nor could both be form. Undoubtedly, one necessarily had to be matter and the other form. For, because non-being does not have a form, it was necessary that being have a form. And because being had to be limited and yet because nothing is limited except by form, it was necessary, as a result, that there be a form by which it was limited, because form holds the being of a thing together.[46]

Moreover, because the first active unity does not have *hyle*, it was necessary that the unity that follows after it have *hyle*,[47] for contrary things agree with respect to contraries. And because form has being only by the power of matter, there had to be matter in which it would subsist. [22]

Moreover, because the creator is perfect, he did not wish to create a perfect first product. It is more perfect, however, to create what subsists in something else and that in which something else subsists, namely, a sustainer and a thing sustained, than to create only one of them.[48] And because the creator is sufficient in himself, needing nothing, the created thing, because it is distinct from him, had to be insufficient and needy. And for this reason, because they were two, it was certainly necessary that they should be such that they would mutually need each other and that neither would be perfected except by the other.[49] Therefore, one had to be matter and the other form. For there are three

---

271, l. 8; and V, 29, p. 310, l. 5. For a discussion of Gundissalinus's use of this metaphysical principle in *De processione mundi*, see Eugene Edward Selk, *The Meaning of the Formula 'omne esse ex forma est' in the De Processione Mundi of Dominicus Gundissalinus* (M.A. Thesis, Marquette University, 1966).

[45] Avicebron, *Fons vitae* II, 19, p. 59, ll. 2-3: "For its subsistence, every form must have matter that sustains it."

[46] Avicebron, *Fons vitae* V, 23, p. 300, ll. 18-20: ". . . since being needed to be finite in itself, it is necessary that it be limited by form, because form holds a thing together."

[47] Avicebron, *Fons vitae* V, 23, p. 300, ll. 20-22: ". . . since the first active unity does not have *hyle*, it is necessary that the unity that follows this one consists of *hyle*."

[48] Avicebron, *Fons vitae* V, 25, p. 303, ll. 13-17: "D: Since it was necessary that the receptive created thing be two, why was one of them a sustainer and the other a sustained thing? M: It is proper to majesty to produce perfection. And to produce a sustainer and a sustained thing is more perfect than to produce a sustainer only or a sustained thing only."

[49] I am reading *sustinens* as *sufficiens* and *insustinens* as *insufficiens*, because this is required by the sense of Gundissalinus's argument. "*Sufficiens*" is, moreover, the word Avicebron uses in *Fons vitae* V, 25, p. 303, ll. 21-25 in an argument that parallels Gundissalinus's argument in this passage. "And also," Avicebron says, "since the first maker, high and holy, is sufficient (*sufficiens*) and perfect, it is necessary that the receptive created thing be needy and imperfect and that a sustainer needed a sustained thing and a sustained thing needed a sustainer and that neither of them would be perfect except by the other."

principles of everything begotten: first, an efficient cause; second, that-from-which, and third, that-in-which.[50] That-in-which is named the matter of things, since in the role of a passive mother it is open to all the motions of the male power coming over it. Form, however, is that-from-which, since it fashions that formless neediness by the motions of the active male power into various results. For, in accord with such neediness, form is the ornament of matter. But, since matter is the neediness for form, in every constitution of things matter is first necessary as a sustainer of the constitution of things; later, the result of the work exists by means of form.[51] Hence, matter could not be without form nor form without matter. For it is impossible that one exist without the other, because being is perfected only from the union of both of them.[52] Hence, one is seen to give being to the other, and each is seen to be the cause of the other in order that it may be.

If, however, each gives being to the other, why doesn't each have being in itself? For what does not have being cannot give being to anything. Hence, it should be known that being is said in two ways. For there is [23] being in potency, which is proper to the essence of each matter by itself and of each form by itself, and there is being in act, which is proper simultaneously to matter and form when they are united together. For it is impossible that matter by itself or form by itself be said to be in the same way as it is said to be when one is united to the other. For, when they are understood in union, that being that is proper to them as united belongs to them, because from the union of them there is necessarily and simultaneously produced some form that was not before in each of them without the other. For from the union of any different things there arises a form that was not before in either of the two things. Hence,

[50] Hermann of Carinthia, *De essentiis* I: "There are three principles of all *genitura* in the opinion of philosophers. First is the efficient cause; second is that as the result of which anything is made; third is that in which anything is made" (p. 77).

[51] Hermann of Carinthia, *De essentiis* I: "Moreover, that in which, or from which, something is made, since it lies open to every movement, as if taking on the role of the mother [*mater*] which is receptive to the covering virtue [of the male], is rightly called the matter [*materia*] of things. Form, however, is that 'as the result of which,' since it moulds that formless necessity by the movements of its property as the active element into various actualisations. For thus according to Hermes the Persian: 'Form is the adornment (*ornatus*) of matter, whereas matter is the necessity of form,' since, in the constitution of each thing, in the first place the sustainer is necessary, then the final stage is the actualisation and the perfection of the work" (pp. 77 and 79; parentheses added). Thus, in calling form the ornament (*ornatus*) of matter in this passage, Gundissalinus is borrowing from Hermann who is himself quoting someone else, namely, Hermes the Persian. This will happen again below, when Gundissalinus refers to Augustine and Apuleius while discussing the incorporeal substances.

[52] Avicebron, *Fons vitae* IV, 10, p. 234, ll. 11-12: ". . . it is not possible that form be without matter, because being is perfected only from the union of them."

the being of matter without form or of form without matter is understood in one way, and the being of matter and form when united is understood in another way.[53] For the being of each of them by itself is being in potency, but the being of them when united is being in act. Hence, before being united, both have being in potency. But, when one is united to the other, both are brought forth from potency to act.

Hence, although it is said that form comes to preexisting matter,[54] matter, nonetheless, by no means preceded first form in time or causality. For, since being comes from form, matter without form certainly could not exist for a moment.[55] Nor did matter precede form with respect to causality, and form is rather for matter the cause of existing in order that it may be. For everything by which something exists is the cause of what exists because of it. And because being exists only by reason of form, matter never existed without form. But because form exists only by reason of the existence of formed matter, it is impossible, for this reason, that form exists [24] without matter, since being is achieved only through the union of both of them.[56] For being, as the philosophers define it, is nothing other than the existence of form in matter.[57] Therefore, neither has being without the other. For, if form without matter has being and yet every being is distinct from that whose being it is, there is certainly some distinction between a form and its being. Moreover, since that being comes from form—for all being comes from form—then that form either has being or not, and it will go on in this way to infinity. But if form

---

[53] This passage concerning the distinction between being in potency and being in act and the different senses in which matter and form exist in potency and in act closely parallels Avicebron's discussion in *Fons vitae* V, 9, pp. 273-274, ll. 13-4.

[54] Avicebron, *Fons vitae* V, 42, p. 335, ll. 7-10: "D: . . . why is form said to come to matter, and from where does form come to matter? M: Form comes from above, and matter receives it from below . . . ."

[55] Avicebron, *Fons vitae* V, 42, p. 334, ll. 9-13: "Matter did not exist without form for the blink of an eye so that it is not created and does not have being. But it was created with form simultaneously, because it had being only by form, that is, because it was created with the creation of the form sustained in it without an interval of time."

[56] Avicebron, *Fons vitae* IV, 10, p. 234, ll. 10-12: "If form exists only by means of the existence of formed matter, then it is not possible that form be without matter, because being is perfected only from the union of them."

[57] This conception of being, namely, that being is nothing other than the existence of form in matter (*esse nihil aliud est quam existentia formae in materia*), also appears in Gundissalinus's *De unitate*: "Hence, philosophers describe it in this way, saying being is the existence of form with matter" (p. 3, ll. 12-14). This conception of being is also found, however, in Avicebron's *Fons vitae* V, 10, p. 274, ll. 18-19, where Avicebron also attributes it to others: "And on account of this, they described being, saying that being is the existence of form in matter." It is unclear to whom Gundissalinus and Avicebron are referring.

without matter or matter without form is said to have being, it is by no means declared to exist. But all of this is understood with respect to actual being.[58]

If, however, someone says that material being preceded formal being—for everything that begins to be in act was, of course, possible before, and for this reason the possibility of matter preceded the being of form—we say in response to this that, just as neither exists in act before the other, so neither exists in potency before the other.[59] For from the moment there began to be the possibility of matter's existing through form, from the same moment there began to be the possibility, even the possibility in matter, of existing through form. Hence, just as they existed in act simultaneously, so they do not precede each other in possibility.

Therefore, these two, namely, matter and form, are the first principles of all beings that have a beginning and the ultimate limit of all beings, with the exception of the creator of them.[60] But they are the first principles in composition and the ultimate limit in resolution, since, just as they are the first from which every composition begins, [25] so they are the last in which every resolution ends. Nothing precedes them except the creator alone, not in time but in causality and eternity.

Although, therefore, one does not precede the other in time or causality, either in being in act or being in potency, form is nonetheless said to give being to matter,[61] and matter is not said to give being to form. The reason for this is this. At the coming of form, matter passes from potency to act. Being in potency, however, is considered like non-being in comparison to that being that is in act. Being in act, then, is first attained when matter is united to form. Therefore, on account of this primacy, matter is not seen to give being to form, but form is seen to give being to matter.

Moreover, matter always remains, but form comes and goes, although not every form. And because form, by coming, constitutes and, by going, destroys

---

[58] That is, form without matter or matter without form has only potential being, not actual being, which is produced when form and matter are united and exist together.

[59] The distinction to which Gundissalinus is referring here, namely, the distinction between material being (*materiale esse*) and formal being (*formale esse*), is made by Avicebron in *Fons vitae* V, 11, pp. 276-277, ll. 24-20.

[60] Avicebron, *Fons vitae* V, 1, p. 257, ll. 14-15: ". . . universal matter and universal form are the farthest limit of all the things that were created . . . ."

[61] Avicebron frequently says that form gives being to matter. See, for instance, *Fons vitae* IV, 10, p. 234, l. 13; V, 9, p. 273, l. 10; V, 23, p. 300, ll. 10-11; and V, 31, p. 314, ll. 12-13, where he says: "Form acts on matter, because it perfects it and gives it being."

what is formed by it, just as the body is destroyed when the soul has been removed, being is for this reason attributed more to form than to matter.[62]

Whatever is made, moreover, has a beginning from matter but is perfected by form. The perfection of a thing, however, is of greater worth than the beginning of a thing. Therefore, form is of greater worth than matter, because matter gives the beginning of a thing, whereas form gives its consummation.

In the following way, however, it is proved that matter preexists and form comes to it. Everything that is made, before it is made, can be made.[63] For, if it were not, at first, able to be made, then it could not be made and, thus, never would be made. Therefore, the possibility of being of everything that was made preceded its being in act. But the possibility of being comes only from matter, whereas the act of being comes from form. For a thing is truly said to be in act when form is judged to have been united to matter. In this way, therefore, in the constitution of a thing matter exists before and form comes to it. And matter gives a beginning to things, but form gives perfection to things. [26]

Hence, although neither is proved to have being in act except by reason of the other, matter is, nonetheless, not said to give being to form, but form is said to give being to matter. This is why matter is said to desire form and to be moved to receive it by the motion, that is, of the natural appetite, by which all things desire to be one.[64] For they can be one only by means of form.

Moreover, every imperfect thing naturally desires to be perfected. But matter without form is imperfect since it is in potency alone. It is then perfected, however, when it is united to form. For this reason, matter naturally desires form because, by means of it, it passes from potency to act, from non-being to being, and from imperfection to perfection.[65] And for this reason it is said that all being comes from form—being in act, not being in potency. For matter without form and form without matter has being in potency. But being in act

---

[62] Avicebron, *Fons vitae* V, 9, pp. 272-273, ll. 26-3: ". . . form is the essence of a thing, and when form is removed, what was formed by it is destroyed because it was the essence of the thing, just like the body is destroyed when the soul has been removed from the body."

[63] Avicebron, *Fons vitae* III, 10, p. 100, ll. 20-21: "Whatever began to be, before it existed, was able to be."

[64] Avicebron, *Fons vitae* V, 32, p. 317, ll. 13-18: "D: What sign is there that the motion of matter and other substances is a desire and love? M: Since the meaning of desire and love is only the searching for the attachment to the thing loved and the union of the lover with it and since matter seeks to be attached to form, it is necessary that its motion be on account of the love and desire that it has for form."

[65] Avicebron, *Fons vitae* V, 26, p. 305, ll. 17-21: "M: . . . matter is in potency, but form is in act and perfection. D: How is this? M: Because matter was not perfect nor did it have being except by form; and on account of this, it was moved at first to receive it, that is to say, to have perfection."

is called being only from form, since a thing is reduced from potency to act only when form is united to matter.

This is also understood in another way. For everything that exists is either sensible or intelligible. But sensation is united only to a sensible form, and the intellect is united only to an intelligible form. For nothing is naturally united to anything except to what is similar to it. For sensible and intelligible forms are positioned in the middle between the form of an intelligence and of a soul and the modes [of existence] of sensible and intelligible forms. But because forms are united [27] only with forms, since they agree with them on account of the likeness that they have between themselves as members of the same genus, an intelligence and a soul apprehend the being of a thing only by means of its forms.[66] And for this reason, not only does all being come from form, but being is also known from form. Therefore, if all being comes from form, form assuredly is not being. For whatever comes from something else is not the thing from which it comes. But all being comes from form. Therefore, no being is form, and no form is being. For being is something that inseparably accompanies form.[67] For, when form comes to matter, it is necessary that there be being in act.

[66] Avicebron, *Fons vitae* IV, 5, p. 221, ll. 14-23: "M: . . . being is either sensible or intelligible, and sensation and the intellect come upon only a sensible or an intelligible form. D: What is the reason for this? M: The reason for this is this, that sensible forms and intelligible forms are inserted between understood forms and sensed forms and the matters that sustain sensible forms and the matters that sustain intelligible forms. And on account of this, forms are united only with forms, because they are united with each other, meet each other, and especially because they are harmonious and under one genus." Also see *Fons vitae* V, 8, p. 271, ll. 9-19: "D: What sign is there that the being of a thing comes only from form? M: A sign of this is that what exists is either sensible or intelligible. And sensation and the intellect are joined only to a sensible or an intelligible form, because sensible and intelligible forms stand in the middle between the form of an intelligence and of a soul and the matters of sensible and intelligible forms; and on account of this, forms are united only with forms, because they are what meets them. — And also, because an intelligence and a soul apprehend a thing only by means of its forms, and forms are united only with forms on account of their likeness and agreement in one genus."

[67] In *Fons vitae* IV, 10 and 11, Avicebron argues for the point Gundissalinus is trying to establish here, namely, that being is not form but arises with the coming of form. In *Fons vitae* IV, 10, p. 234, ll. 13-19, Avicebron says: "D: Since form gives being to matter, why will it not have being by itself? M: If you give being to form and ascribe it to it, will you, in doing that, say that the concept of form is the concept of being or something else? D: I am saying that the concept of being is the concept of form. M: How will one of them be the other, since one is a property of the other?" Being is, then, a property of form, and so, being is not form, which, on the other hand, is unity or oneness. Thus, in *Fons vitae* IV, 11, p. 235, ll. 16-29, Avicebron says: "D: . . . . But, by means of a clear display, show in another way that

Since, therefore, all being comes from form but between being and non-being there is nothing in the middle, matter without form is seen to be a privation. Hence, certain people called it a lack (*carentiam*). But it should not, nonetheless, be called a privation unqualifiedly because it has some being in itself, namely, being in potency. For being in act, which matter in itself has only when it is understood to be united to form, is removed from matter when it is considered only in itself. Given the removal of its being, matter alone can be called a privation, not, nonetheless, a privation unqualifiedly. For a privation in the unqualified sense, concerning which there is no previous knowledge, cannot go forth into being. But matter, when it is understood by itself without form, has being in potency, namely, that being which it has in the wisdom of the creator. In fact, the being of matter is in the wisdom of the creator just as the being of the concept of matter is in my soul, which, even if it is in privation with respect to [28] you, is not, nonetheless, in privation with respect to me.[68]

---

form is unity. M: Behold the properties of unity, because you will find them attached to form. This is because unity produces multitude, preserves it, gives it being, holds it together, and exists in all the parts of it, sustained in it because multitude is subjected to it, and unity is of greater worth because multitude is subjected to it. Similarly, these properties are found in form, because form constitutes the essence of that in which it exists, acquires being for it, preserves it, holds it together, and exists in all the parts of it, sustained in the matter subjected to it, it being higher and matter being below it. When you knew these properties, use each of them as a middle term between form and unity, and from this, the necessary proof demonstrating that form is unity will be completed for you." Hence, according to Avicebron, being is not form but arises with the coming of form, which, by contrast, is unity or oneness. Below, Gundissalinus too maintains that form is unity or oneness.

[68] Avicebron, *Fons vitae* V, 10, pp. 274-275, ll. 8-3: "D: From your words, I conclude that matter is privation. For, since the being of a thing is only on account of form and between being and non-being there is not a medium, it is necessary that matter itself be privation. M: Even if matter is said to be in privation, it, nonetheless, must not be said that it does not have some being in itself besides the being that it has when it is joined to form, that is, being in potency. And on account of this, it is said that matter does not have being in act unqualifiedly, because it has being in itself in potency, and being in act is [found] only when matter is joined to form. And on account of this, they described being, saying that being is the existence of form in matter. Similarly, matter is not in privation unqualifiedly, because it has being in itself in potency, that is, that being that it had in the knowledge of the eternal, exalted and great one, not composed with form. D: Explain this notion to me further, namely, the being of matter without form in the wisdom of the exalted and great creator. M: The being of matter in the wisdom of God is just as the being, in my soul, of a concept about which you inquire, because, even if it is in privation with respect to you, it, nonetheless, must not be in privation with respect to me."

And on account of this being, namely, being in potency, which is now nothing, matter is said to desire and to be moved towards form. For nothing is moved except in order to have something that it lacks. To have that which it lacks, however, is to be perfected by it. But matter is perfected by form. Matter is, therefore, moved in order to have form in order that it may be perfected by it.[69] Matter, therefore, has some being without form, namely, being in potency. For, if it existed in no way, it would not be said to be moved in order to have form. Similarly, form without matter has being in potency.

Hence, it is not absurd that each of them without the other has being and non-being simultaneously, but in a different way. For material being, which is being in potency, is distinct from formal being, which is being in act. But each of them by itself without the other has material being, just as each of them has formal being if it is united with the other. But because men have not been accustomed to say that something exists except what exists in act, while being in act is present only when form is united to matter, being does not belong to matter by itself nor to form by itself, but to both of them [29] when joined together. And therefore, whatever is composed of matter and form has in a similar fashion being that is composed of being in potency, which is material being, and being in act, which is formal being.[70]

But because being and oneness are inseparable—since whatever exists exists because it is one[71]—just as neither has being by itself without the other, so neither is one by itself without the other. For whatever exists is either one or many. Therefore, because it is neither one nor many, matter in itself understood without form and form understood without matter cannot be called one.

---

[69] Avicebron, *Fons vitae* V, 10, p. 275, ll. 23-28: ". . . the motion of a thing that is moved is only so that it may have and be perfected by it; and whatever is moved to something lacks it. From this, therefore, it follows that first matter, since it is moving so that its motion is for the sake of something else, namely, form, so that it may have it and be perfected by it, needed at first to have lacked it."

[70] I am reading *quicquid est non compositum ex materia et forma* without *non*, because this is required by the sense of the argument. This reading is required, moreover, by the parallel text from Avicebron's *Fons vitae* V, 11, p. 277, ll. 5-9: "And also, when you consider that the being of a thing composed of matter and form is composed from being in potency, which is the being of matter, and being in act, which is the being of form, you will see that the being of matter in comparison with that is a privation."

[71] This metaphysical principle, namely, that everything that exists exists precisely because it is one (*omne quod est ideo est quia unum est*), also appears in Gundissalinus's *De unitate*: "Hence, it is that whatever exists exists precisely because it is one" (p. 3, ll. 8-9). Yet, in *Fons vitae* V, 9, p. 273, ll. 3-5, Avicebron likewise maintains that a thing has being only because of oneness or unity: ". . . unity is the cause of a thing itself, because a thing is called itself, that is, because it has being, only on account of unity, which constitutes its essence."

For, because oneness is form,[72] if matter without form were one, then matter without form would certainly be matter with form, which is impossible. And because all being is called one, it is not possible that oneness exists in non-being.[73] Hence, neither matter nor form had being in act before oneness, but they began to be simultaneously. For, when form was united to matter, oneness instantly came forth, because from the union of them something one is made. Hence, being and oneness are seen to be simultaneous by nature since, when [30] something exists, it is one, and when it is one, it necessarily is. And consequently, just as matter without form or form without matter does not have being, so neither without the other is one by means of oneness.

And when, nonetheless, philosophers describe first matter and form, they say: First matter is a substance existing through itself, the sustainer of diversity and one in number. Moreover, first matter is a substance receptive to all forms. First form, however, is a substance constituting the essence of all forms.[74] Although, however, one is shown to differ from the other by this and yet every difference is by means of form, it should not be said, nonetheless, that one differs from the other by something different from themselves. On the contrary, each one differs from the other by itself, not by a difference that belongs to things in agreement, but one that belongs to opposition and true contrariety, since each of them is other than the other.[75] For, if substantiality and oneness are forms, then, since each of them is said of a substance that is one in number, matter in itself is certainly not entirely formless, and form is not entirely simple, since substantiality and oneness are properties of them. Hence, it must not be said that substantiality and oneness are forms of matter and form

[72] At least twice in the *Fons vitae*, Avicebron says that oneness or unity is form: *Fons vitae* IV, 11, p. 236, l. 6: ". . . oneness is form alone . . ;" and *Fons vitae* V, 9, p. 272, l. 19: ". . . oneness is form . . . ." Conversely, in addition to the above-cited text from *Fons vitae* IV, 11, p. 235, ll. 16-29, Avicebron says that form is oneness or unity in at least two other texts: *Fons vitae* IV, 10, p. 234, l. 23: ". . . form is only oneness;" and *Fons vitae* IV, 13, p. 240, l. 11: ". . . form is oneness . . . ."

[73] Avicebron, *Fons vitae* V, 9, p. 272, ll. 13-14: ". . . being is called one, and it is not possible that oneness exists in non-being . . . ."

[74] Avicebron, *Fons vitae* V, 22, p. 298, ll. 13-19: "Therefore, the description of first matter that is taken from its properties is this, namely, that it is a substance existing through itself, the sustainer of diversity [that is] one in number; and again, it will be described in this way, that it is the substance receptive to all forms. But the description of universal form is this, namely, that it is a substance constituting the essence of all forms."

[75] Avicebron, *Fons vitae* V, 2, p. 260, ll. 12-17: "D: In what does matter differ from form, when the essence of each of them is considered? M: Each of them differs from the other by itself. And I do not mean here a difference of things in agreement, but I mean a difference of opposition and true contrariety, because there is not something above them in which they agree."

as if they were different from them, but [31] they are matter and form, not something other than them.

Nor is matter, which sometimes is called "matter" and sometimes "substance," something other than substance. For it is called "matter" when it is referred to form, but it is called "substance" when it is considered by itself.[76] For matter itself is called by different names when it is viewed in different respects. For, from the fact that it is in potency as receptive of forms, it is called "*hyle*," and from the fact that it is already in act as sustaining form, it is called "subject." But, when a substance is described, "subject" is not understood in the same sense as it is in logic. For *hyle* is not a subject in this way, but it is a subject of form. And from the fact that it is common to all forms, it is called either "mass" or "matter." And from the fact that other things are broken down into it, since it is the simple part of every composite, it is called "element," and it is the same way in other things. And from the fact that composition begins from it, it is called "origin." But, when we begin with a composite and come to it, it is called "element."[77]

Form also does not seem to be substance. For the property of a substance is existence by itself.[78] But form cannot exist by itself because it has being in act only in matter. Hence, because it needs matter for its being, certain people called it "accidental," not nonetheless "an accident." [79] But because all being

---

[76] Avicebron, *Fons vitae* V, 7, p. 269, ll. 18-21: ". . . the essence itself of substance is the essence of matter, and they are distinguished by name only when they are considered in different respects. Therefore, it is called 'matter' when it is referred to form, and it is called 'substance' when it stands by itself."

[77] It is from Avicenna that Gundissalinus borrows the different names that may be applied to matter when it is viewed in different respects. In *Physics* I, 2, Avicenna says that ". . . a natural body, from the fact that it is a body, has a principle which is *hyle* and a principle which is form . . . ." The Latin text of this passage, which I have translated for this note, is on p. 21, ll. 50-51 of *Avicenna Latinus: Liber primus naturalium: Tractatus primus De causis et principiis naturalium*, édition critique de la traduction latine médiévale par Simone van Riet, introduction doctrinale par G. Verbeke (Louvain: E. Peeters; Leiden: E.J. Brill, 1992). References to this work will be as follows: Avicenna, *Physics*, with the book, chapter(s), page(s), and line number(s) in Van Riet's edition. In all cases, the translation is mine. While subsequently distinguishing the different senses in which *hyle*, that is, matter, may be considered, Avicenna discusses matter considered as *hyle*, a subject, mass, an element, and an origin, as Gundissalinus does here. See Avicenna, *Physics* I, 2, pp. 21-22, ll. 60-69.

[78] Avicebron, *Fons vitae* V, 23, p. 300, ll. 2-3: ". . . the property of a substance is that it exists by itself."

[79] Gundissalinus is probably referring to Avicebron, who, in the following text from *Fons vitae* V, 22, pp. 298-299, ll. 22-5, argues that, although first form is accidental when it is considered in relation to the matter that sustains it, first form is not an accident: "D: How is first form called 'substance' since it is sustained in matter?

comes from form, but being does not come from an accident but in another way, form is, therefore, not an accident. But it is a substance, because [32] whatever exists is a substance or an accident.

Plato says, nonetheless, that first matter was between some substance and no substance and rightly, since, between complete being and complete non-being, it is possible for a substance to be in between.[80] And for this reason, matter, which before being united with form was in potency only, is said to have been between no substance and some substance so that it may be understood to have been only the possibility of being. For the name of substance properly belongs to that matter that has already received some form through which it was made a substance. Hence, it is called "substance" because it stands under some form.[81] First matter, therefore, was not some substance, because in itself and by reason of itself it had no form. For its own form makes any substance be. But it was not any substance because every form was in it potentially, and it itself was receptive in potency to all forms. Hence, by others, it is even called substance in the way in which an egg is said to be an animal. For an egg is not an animal in act, but only in potency, that is, in the substance of the egg there is matter or possibility or potency or a suitability that an animal may be produced from it by generation. Hence, we cannot simply deny that an egg is an animal or simply affirm that it is, since it is an animal in potency, and this

---

M: Certainly, form is accidental when it is considered with respect to its being sustained in matter; but in itself it is a substance. And therefore they called this form 'substantial' and not 'substance' unqualifiedly. And in general, since an accident is not an accident only on account of its being sustained but on account of the fact that it is destroyed after it is separated from the thing sustaining it, first form must not be an accident for the reason that it is sustained in matter."

[80] Though Gundissalinus here refers to Plato, Bülow suggests that he is not referring to any Platonic text but, instead, to either Apuleius's *Plato and his Doctrine* or Chalcidius's *Commentary on the Timaeus of Plato*. Bülow says: "Den Plato und Aristoteles erwähnt Dominicus in unserem Traktat, wird aber von ersterem gar nichts . . . ; über Plato könnte er auch vielleicht etwas in Apuleius, '*De Platone et eius dogmate*' oder auch in Chalcidius, '*In Timaeum*,' gelesen haben" (Introduction, p. XIX). I have not been able to determine the Platonic text, if any, Gundissalinus has in mind here. He may be thinking of Plato's discussion of the receptacle at *Timaeus* 48e2-52d2. As Bülow has suggested, however, Gundissalinus may be thinking of Apuleius's discussion of matter in *Plato and his Doctrine* I, 5. For, in that text, Apuleius claims that, according to Plato, matter is neither a corporeal substance nor an incorporeal substance.

[81] Avicebron, *Fons vitae* II, 11, p. 42, ll. 20-24: "This distinction of names, namely, of 'substance' and 'matter,' exists because the name 'matter' fits that alone that is prepared to receive a form that it has not yet received, whereas the name 'substance' fits that matter that already received some form and, through that form, was made a true substance."

mode of being is in between being and non-being.[82] Matter in itself, therefore, is only the possibility of being. [33]

The question arises about this possibility whether it is something or nothing, that is, only an empty sound without any meaning. For, if the possibility of being is absolutely nothing, then, when matter is said to be possibility,[83] it is said to be absolutely nothing, and those who endeavor to discuss matter speak about nothing. If, however, it is something, then it was a substance or an accident. But because possibility is relative to what can be—for possibility is only something possible, and something possible is possible only by means of possibility—it seems to be an accident. If, however, it is an accident, then it is necessary that it have a subject in which it subsists. But there existed only God, in whom there can be no accident. It could not, therefore, be an accident, because it had nothing in which to subsist. It was, therefore, a substance. But, because it was between no substance and some substance, it was certainly neither a substance nor an accident. For this division is found only in natural things.

Moreover, in the following way the question arises about this possibility, which is matter, whether it began to be or not. For whatever begins to be, before it begins to be, is only in potency, that is, before it begins. After all, it can begin to be. For, if it could not begin to be, it certainly never would begin to be. The possibility of being, therefore, precedes that being. But matter considered by itself without form existed only in potency. Therefore, either it did or did not begin to be in potency. If, however, it did not begin to be in potency, then it was a being in potency without a beginning. But the being of matter by itself is being in potency. The being of matter, therefore, is without a beginning. Therefore, matter in itself is eternal. What is eternal, however, or what exists and did not begin to be was not created. [34] Created being, however, began to be. Hence, because matter does not begin to be, it was created neither from nothing nor from something. If, however, it began to be in potency, but the possibility of being in any way precedes everything that began to be in some way—for it would not exist in that way unless, before, it was possible that it be in that way—then the possibility of being in potency preceded matter's

---

[82] On pp. 164-165 of "Las fuentes literarias de Domingo Gundisalvo," *Al-Andalus* 11 (1946): 159-173, Alonso shows that Gundissalinus here borrows from *The Exalted Faith* of Abraham ibn Daud the example of an egg and the animal generated from it in order to explain the sense in which first matter is a substance.

[83] In at least two texts, Avicebron refers to matter as possibility: *Fons vitae* V, 24, p. 303, l. 3: ". . . first matter is rightly called 'possibility' . . ;" and *Fons vitae* V, 42, p. 334, ll. 18-21: "D: . . . . But philosophers are in the habit of calling matter 'possibility.' M: They called matter 'possibility' only because it was possible for it to receive form . . . ."

being in potency. And similarly, it could be asked about that possibility if it began to be, and so on to infinity.

It was said before, moreover, that the being in potency of matter is its being in the wisdom of the creator. But nothing begins to be in the wisdom of the creator, for then something new would happen to him, which is impossible. Matter, therefore, did not begin to be in potency. It was, therefore, in potency without a beginning, because it was in the wisdom of the creator without a beginning.

Therefore, according to material being, which is being in potency, matter did not begin to be. And the same is true of form. Hence, that "being that was made was life in him."[84] It seems, however, that matter began according to formal being. For, because creation is the acquisition of being, but being comes only from form, for matter to be created was nothing other than for it to be united to form. After all, it was never true that matter existed and had not been or was not united with form. For they were created simultaneously, because they began to be simultaneously when they were united to each other.[85] For, since matter and form are opposites and since opposites are in themselves united to each other only by something else—but matter and form have being only by means of their union with each other—[then], certainly, their being united to each other was their being created from nothing. [35] For, because things have being by creation only from their opposite, it is necessary that being comes from its privation, that is, from non-being. And consequently, matter comes from non-matter and form from non-form. Privation, however, is nothing. Therefore, matter and form are said to be created from nothing. For, because the creator alone existed, they certainly could be created only from him or from nothing. What is from him, however, is nothing other than him, but is the same as he is and, therefore, was neither made nor created, but was generated or proceeds.[86] These things, however, are other than him; hence, they are not from him, but were created from nothing, since there was nothing from which they could be created. If, however, matter and form were made by generation—and yet everything natural is made from what is similar to it—

---

[84] John 1: 14.

[85] Avicebron, *Fons vitae* V, 42, p. 334, ll. 6-13: "D: It is now clear, from what has preceded, that matter does not have being. And creation is the acquisition of being. Hence, it follows that matter is not created. M: Matter was not without form for the blink of an eye so that it is not created and does not have being. But it was created with form simultaneously, because it did not have being except from form, that is, because it was made with the creation of the form sustained in it without an interval of time."

[86] Hermann of Carinthia, *De essentiis* I: "For whatever comes out of or of Himself, that same thing is God, and thus is not made by God, but is generated or proceeds from Him" (p. 87).

then this would go on to infinity. For this reason, matter and form do not have being by generation. And therefore, each of them was simple, because nothing from which they might be made preceded the principles whose creation was the first motion, since no motion preceded it. But creation preceded every motion not in time, but in causality.

We inquire into this motion of creation in the following way. Only possible being is made. But when it is made, everything that is a possible being goes forth from potency to act. Therefore, everything that is made goes forth from potency to act. But to go forth from potency to act is nothing other than to be moved from potency to act. For every going forth is a motion. However, because it is moved from potency to act, it is not yet in act. For nothing is moved to that state in which it exists. To be moved from potency to act, therefore, is prior to being in act. Nothing, however, is in act except by means of form, for all being comes from form. Hence, to be moved to being in act is nothing other than to be moved to being by means of form. To be moved to form, therefore, is prior to being by means of form. But form is in it only because it exists by means of it. What [36] exists by means of form, however, is moved to it before it has being by means of it. But creation is a motion to being by means of form. The motion of creation, therefore, is seen to precede every form and, thus, everything that has being by means of form. Therefore, these two, namely, first matter and first form, are prior to all the things that have a beginning, because these alone have being by creation. Other things, however, have a beginning either by their union or by generation or by the commingling of generated things.

Theologians, nonetheless, and certain of the poets say that first matter was a kind of blending and mixture of things.[87] In this blending of things, this earthy element resides in one and the same middle place and endowed with a better form than the other elements mixed together in the one blending, but is wrapped all around by those other elements like an opaque cloud so that what it was could not be seen. The other three elements, however, which were mixed and blended with one another and suspended all around it, were stretched out upwards to where the summit of corporeal creation now ends. This whole space that stretches from the surface of the earth, which is positioned in the middle, all the way to the edge of the highest sphere, was filled with that darkness and cloud. And the riverbeds or paths of the waters that now exist were then surely prepared in the body of the earth as future receptacles for these

---

[87] As I noted in the Introduction, Alonso has shown, in "Hugo de San Victor refutado por Domingo Gundisalvo hacia el 1170," *Estudios eclesiásticos* 21 (1947): 209-216, that one of the theologians Gundissalinus has in mind in the following passage is Hugh of St. Victor. When, on the other hand, Gundissalinus refers to "certain of the poets," he has Ovid in mind, as will become evident below.

waters. In those times, that great abyss from which the streams of all waters flowed was also still an open and empty chasm, and a horrendous void stretched straight downward over which the clouds of that gloomy darkness by which the whole surface of the earth was then covered were stretched out from above. It is these clouds, so they say, [37] that Divine Scripture testifies to as having been upon the face of the deep when heaven and earth were created.[88]

The surface of the world is said to have been created as such in the beginning, before it received form and distinction into different kinds of things. In this way, it was created, as it were, formless in the same place where now it subsists as formed. When Moses says, "In the beginning, God created heaven and earth,"[89] by "heaven" and "earth" in this statement he wanted us to understand the matter of all heavenly and earthly things from which, afterwards, those things were subsequently distinguished by means of form which were earlier created at the same time in themselves through their essence. When, however, he then adds, "The earth was empty and void,"[90] "earth" signifies the element of earth. And "heaven" was that moving and light blend of the remaining three elements, which, being suspended, were carried on a course around the earth that was positioned in the middle. Then his words, "and darkness was upon the face of the deep"[91] and the others that follow, add further descriptions to the previously mentioned description. A poet also agrees with this, saying

there was one countenance to all of nature in the world, which was called chaos, an undeveloped and disorderly mass.[92]

But according to the philosophers, who hold that an angelic creature consists of matter and form, this chaos does not seem to have been the first [38] matter of all creatures.[93] For this matter could not, of course, have been something spiritual, because it was a body, and because they say that it was a mixture of both the elements and things composed of the elements, from which the heavenly bodies were distinguished through the distinction of their form, they seem to contradict the philosophers who testify that the heavenly bodies came, not from the elements, but from first matter.[94]

In the following way, however, it is seen to be proved that that blending of things was not first matter. The elements are composed of matter and form,[95]

---

[88] Genesis 1:2.
[90] Genesis 1:2.
[92] Ovid, *Metamorphoses* I, ll. 6-7.
[93] The precise sources are unclear.
[94] The precise sources are unclear.
[95] In *Fons vitae* I, 14, p. 17, ll. 3-17, Avicebron contends that the elements, along with all sensible things, are composed of matter and form: "D: Now, therefore, make clear the being of universal matter and universal form together according to

[89] Genesis 1:1.
[91] Ibid.

for the elements are bodies because they are limited and have qualities. However, whatever things are composed of some other things are posterior to the things of which they are composed. Matter and form, therefore, are prior to the elements. But that chaos was a mixture of the elements and things composed of the elements. For this reason, that chaos was not created from nothing, since it was a mixture from many bodies. For a thing that is seen to be composed of so many things is not said to have been created from nothing. For this reason, that chaos could not have been first matter, because the creation of those simple things preceded it, although not by time, but by causality.

Moreover, whatever is broken down into other things comes after the things into which it is broken down. But that chaos is broken down into the elements and the elements into the things composed of the elements, while the things composed of the elements are broken down into matter and form. Since, therefore, that chaos is posterior to many bodies, it certainly could not have been the matter of all bodies.

Therefore, first matter and first form are quite fittingly said to be those things [39] than which nothing is seen to be prior except their creator. Their union was the first composition. For the first composition is the union of first form with first matter, and this union is a certain limited relation of form uniting with matter from which the generation of all things arises as from the union of a male and a female. [96] For, because matter is only receptive and not active, form is only active and not receptive. After all, form acts on matter since it alone perfects it and gives it being in act. But matter does not have any action since in itself it is only receptive, that is, suited only to receive the action of form. [97]

---

the proper way, which you discussed before, because it is already evident to me according to the common way. M: Consider universal and particular natural sensible things, and you will not find in them another besides these. D: What is an example of this in particular things? M: Animals, vegetables, and inanimate things each are composed of matter and form. D: It is so. M: Also consider particular artificial things, such as a statue and a bed. D: I already examined them, and I again found it to be so. M: It is also this way in the universal natural things, which are the four elements."

[96] Hermann of Carinthia, *De essentiis* I: "The principal movement of these is, therefore, the generation of all things. For that movement is a certain regulated *habitudo* of form coming together with matter . . ." (p. 79).

[97] Avicebron, *Fons vitae* V, 31, p. 314, ll. 10-15: "D: . . . make me know whether form acts on matter or matter on form. M: Form acts on matter, because it perfects it and gives it being. And matter does not have action, because its being is under the control of [form], for in itself it is only receptive alone, that is, subjected to or prepared to receive action."

For this reason philosophers call form "a man" and matter "a woman," since whatever is in act is generated from preexisting matter and an active form as from the union of a male and a female.[98]

The first union of form with matter is like the union of light with air[99] or of the soul with the body or of heat with quantity and of quantity with a substance, and it is like the union of the intellect with the object understood and of the sense with the object sensed.[100] And the sending forth (*emissio*) of form into matter by God, which is just as [the motion] from non-being to being, is just like the sending forth of the understanding from its own essence upon the thing understood or just like the sending forth of the sense to the thing sensed.[101] [40] The union of form with matter is compared to the union of light with air for this reason that, just as a dark thing is seen by means of light, so what the thing itself is is known by means of form. For, if a thing is known when its being is understood and yet being comes only from form, knowledge of a thing is certainly attained only by means of form. Hence, since matter in itself is taken to be formless, it is almost not understood, since knowledge of no thing is attained except by means of form. Hence, form is fittingly called the ornament and light of matter, because, just as light is accustomed to make clear the form of a thing and to reveal its hiddenness, so matter becomes manifest through form without which it lies hidden in potency. And because the Word is an intelligible light by means of whose gaze form is impressed into

[98] The precise sources are unclear. But, in *Generation of Animals* I, 20, 729a24-33, Aristotle discusses the way in which form, which is active, is like a male and matter, which is passive and receptive, is like a female.

[99] Avicebron often compares the union of form with matter to the union of light with air. See, for instance, *Fons vitae* IV, 14, p. 241, ll. 20-22; V, 30, p. 313, ll. 9-12; and V, 6, p. 267, ll. 6-7, where he says: "Imagine that the union of form with matter is just like the union of light with air . . . ."

[100] Avicebron, *Fons vitae* V, 27, p. 307, ll. 8-12: "D: Also give an example of how matter and form are united. M: An example of this is the union of light with air, of a color with a subject, of the soul with the body, of the intelligence with the soul, of the sense with the object sensed, and of the intellect with the object understood."

[101] Avicebron, *Fons vitae* V, 6, p. 267, ll. 15-24: "Therefore, the consideration of the union of form with first matter and of its conjoining with it will be just like the consideration of the union of the intelligence with the soul and of the soul with an accident that is sustained in it and with the body with which it is bound together; and what is more subtle and more opaque than this is the union of the intellect with the object understood and of the sense with the object sensed. And according to this example, we will also consider the production of form in matter by God, who is exalted and holy, from privation to being to be just like the sending forth (*emissio*) of the intellect from its own essence upon the thing understood and the sending forth (*emissio*) of the sense upon the thing sensed."

matter, for this reason form, which comes from him, is not unfittingly called light.[102] For all forms reflect here as if in some mirror different likenesses from the simple and first form of the divinity, and certain of these are truly impressed here like images.[103] For the creation of things by the creator is only the going forth of form from his wisdom and will and the impression of his image in matter like the going forth of water emanating from its origin and its flowing out when one part [41] follows after another. But the going forth of water is without interruption and pause, whereas creation is without motion and time. In fact, the sealing of form in matter, when it comes from the divine wisdom, is like the sealing of a shape in a mirror when the shape is reflected in it from one who is looking at it. And, in this way, matter receives form from the divine will, just as a mirror receives a shape from one who is looking into it, and nonetheless, matter does not receive the essence of that from which it receives form, just as the sense does not receive the matter of a sensed thing whose form it receives. For whatever acts upon another acts upon it only by means of its own form, which it impresses on it.[104]

However, the first form to which first matter was joined was substantiality, which made matter be a substance. But because everything that exists exists precisely because it is one, substantiality alone, therefore, could not come to matter without unity as its companion, because it was impossible for matter to become a substance and not one. Hence, substantiality and unity come to matter simultaneously, and at their coming matter passes from possibility to act, from darkness to light, from deformity to comeliness, since by their union matter is made one substance. Hence, those things are rightly called "the firsts,"

---

[102] Avicebron, *Fons vitae* V, 30, p. 313, ll. 13-20: "D: . . . . But explain why they called this form light. M: Since the Word by means of whose gaze form was implanted is light, that is, an intelligible light, not a sensible light, it is necessary that the form implanted by him also be a light. And also, because [just as] light is accustomed to make clear and penetrate the form of a thing and to reveal it after its hiddenness, in the same way form, when it is united with matter, becomes visible by means of it after its own hiddenness, and it has being by means of it."

[103] Hermann of Carinthia, *De essentiis* I: "The ultimate origin of all forms is from the simple and pure form of the Divinity, in which, as it were, all forms are radiated in different reflections from a kind of mirror. In this form, according to the theological tradition, is placed the eternal essence of the forms, so that all other forms are most correctly understood as being, so to speak, certain images of that principal and true form" (p. 111).

[104] The two images Gundissalinus here uses for creation, namely, the flowing of water emanating from its origin and a mirror receiving the shape of one who is looking into it, are also used by Avicebron and in the same order; see *Fons vitae* V, 41, pp. 330-331, ll. 17-7. It is interesting to note, however, that Gundissalinus does not use Avicebron's third image for creation wherein creation is likened to a word spoken by a man; Avicebron uses this image in *Fons vitae* V, 43, pp. 336-337, ll. 1-2.

[because], if they did not bring matter into being by coming in advance, certainly no forms would ever subsist in matter. For, if being a substance is prior to being a corporeal and an incorporeal substance, the corporeity of a substance [42] comes to it in order that it may be a corporeal substance. The same is true about an incorporeal substance. Every accident, however, comes only to a corporeal or an incorporeal substance. Substantiality and unity are certainly the first of all forms, because they come before all forms with respect to causality, and without them no forms suddenly subsist in a subject. They are the first of all forms because, by constituting it and making it appear, they come before to a substance, which is a subject of all [other] forms.

With respect to form, one is spiritual, another corporeal, and another in the middle. — A form is called corporeal that is found only in bodies, as, for example, corporeity, quantity, color, and similar things. There are two sides to a corporeal form: intrinsic condition (*intrinseca habitudo*) and extrinsic completeness (*extrinseca absolutio*). The intrinsic condition consists of the proportion of the mixture (*in commixtionis proportione*) of the components of the body, and the extrinsic completeness consists of the arrangement of the shape (*in figurae dispositione*) of the body.[105] But one corporeal form is substantial, another accidental. That form is called substantial that, when it comes, instantly brings matter forth into being and constitutes its species, as, for example, corporeity, and for this reason it is said to be created from nothing. But a form is called accidental either that is generated from the coming together of matter and form or that is added from the outside. But the forms that are generated from the coming together of matter and form are called compounded. Some of them arise from matter, as, for example, the blackness of an Ethiopian and tallness of stature. Others arise from form, as, for example, cheerfulness and the power of laughing. Others arise from both matter and form and need the union of both, as, for example, sleeping and being awake, although sleeping belongs more to matter and being awake to form. Other forms belong to matter alone without form, as, for example, color. Others belong to form alone without matter, as, for example, knowledge.[106] — [43] Also, a form is called spiritual that is found in spiritual things alone. This form has neither an intrinsic nor an extrinsic side like a corporeal form, because a spirit does not have an inside and an outside, for that is proper to a corporeal substance alone. But one spiritual form is substantial, as, for example,

[105] Hermann of Carinthia, *De essentiis* I: "Every form consists of two parts . . . . These parts are the internal *habitudo* and the external completeness. The internal *habitudo* consists in the proportion of the mixture, but the external completeness is in the disposition of the figure . . ." (p. 111).

[106] Gundissalinus's discussion of accidental corporeal forms closely parallels Avicenna's discussion in *Physics* I, 6, p. 61, ll. 44-58.

rationality, whereas another is accidental, as, for example, knowledge or wisdom. — But a form is called intermediate without which no form is certainly ever found in the subject of either a spiritual or a corporeal substance, as, for example, substantiality and unity.

However, every form or all forms are in matter in potency. In itself, however, matter is receptive to all forms. For this reason, it happened that, when forms came to matter by the command of the creator, as the excellence of each form required and as the aptitude of the parts of matter desired, the various species of things were formed so that the beginnings of form, namely, corporeity and spirituality, came to matter that was already constituted, that is, made into one substance, and distinguished the whole of it completely into two kinds, namely, corporeal and incorporeal substance. Afterwards, the forms accompanying and attendant upon those two kinds subsequently divided them into the many species and orders of things by the ministry of nature. At first, therefore, what is composed of matter and form was divided into corporeal and incorporeal substance.[107]

And corporeal substance, which is body, is divided into body that is an element and into body that is composed only of the elements, as, for example, all sensible things lower than the moon, and into body that is neither an element [44] nor composed of the elements, as, for example, every body that is higher than the moon. According to its distance from the motion of higher things, body that is only an element is divided by the coming to it of hotness, coldness, dryness, and wetness into those first four simple bodies that are called the elements, from which this whole worldly body, namely, this sublunar body, is entirely composed. In fact, their worldly offspring is generated from the mixture and change of them.

But incorporeal substance is divided into rational and irrational. — One rational substance contemplates the divine simplicity, as, for example, the angels; another acts as a minister of the divine disposition of things, as, for example, according to certain people, the spirits of the planets. Another is subject to human neediness, as, for example, the human soul; still another is consigned to eternal damnation and sent into perpetual exile among the waves, winds, and fire within the belly of the sublunar world.[108] This last kind of

---

[107] In this paragraph, Gundissalinus argues that matter becomes one substance and then is distinguished completely into two kinds of substance, namely, corporeal and incorporeal substance. Gundissalinus may have in mind Book I, Chapter 2 of Abraham ibn Daud's *The Exalted Faith* where ibn Daud first discusses prime matter and then claims that substance is divisible into corporeal and incorporeal substance.

[108] While discussing the spirits in Book II of his *De essentiis*, Hermann of Carinthia says: "... part is contemplating the divine simplicity, part is ministering the divine disposition, part also is yielding to the necessities of mankind, but part is con-

rational substance is immortal and is, as Augustine maintains, altogether incorporeal, having an ethereal body that is, because of its simple nature, perfect and, therefore, incorruptible. But Apuleius [45] defined a demon in this way: a demon is an immortal, rational, and airy animate being that can suffer. Hence, demons are said to feel pity, to suffer distress, to be glad, to become angry, to be exposed to all of the affections of the human soul, and to fluctuate through all the turmoil of thoughts by a similar motion of the heart and the billow of the mind.[109] — Irrational substance, however, is divided into nature, the vegetative soul, and the sensitive soul.

But with the exception of the things composed of the elements and the irrational substances, all these things discussed before, since they were generated from the first union of matter and form, which are simple things, are all therefore incorruptible and are called "a lasting offspring" since, from that moment in which they came to be simultaneously [46] begotten, none is ever destroyed by corruption. Hence, no incorporeal substance and no corporeal substance, insofar as it is a body, can be corrupted.[110] For God is incorruptible and immutable as well as those things that he willed to make first. And he bestowed this as a gift in order that they might approach a likeness of him by reason of the fact that they would utterly lack an end. For the eternal one could not create eternal things, because, if it is a creature, then surely it is not eternal. And nonetheless, he made what he could, because from the things to which he gave a beginning through himself he took an end away in order that, since on account of their beginning they cannot wholly have eternity, they might at least have something of eternity in the other direction, since they would be without

---

demned to eternal damnation and, as if deported below the boundary of the sublunary world, and torn apart by earth, waves, winds and flames, is kept in perpetual exile and misery" (p. 185).

[109] Though Gundissalinus refers to Augustine and Apuleius in this passage, references to these two thinkers appear in the text from Book II of Hermann of Carinthia's *De essentiis* that Gundissalinus is using in this passage. Hermann says: "However, all that genus is immortal in that it either is completely incorporeal, or, as Father Augustine writes, has an ethereal body perfected by a simple nature, and hence is without dissolution, and is incorruptible. For Apuleius defines demon, too, as a rational, immortal animal, of air, and capable of suffering . . . . For, he says, 'demons can have compassion and be displeased, they can be vexed and be joyful, they can suffer every state of the human mind with a similar emotion of the heart, and even be tossed on the salt-sea of the mind on every tide of thought . . .'" (pp. 185 and 187). Hermann is referring to Augustine's *The City of God* VIII, ch. 15-16 and to Apuleius's *The God of Socrates*, ch. 12-13.

[110] That is, no rational incorporeal substance can be corrupted; the irrational incorporeal substances can be corrupted, as Gundissalinus indicated in the previous sentence.

every end. Hence, they are perpetual. But the things that come from something perpetual or that are made by something perpetual are closed in at each end, because just as they have a beginning by generation, so they receive an end by corruption. In this way, therefore, the product of the eternal one is perpetuated as a perpetual product just as the product of nature is by a temporal one so that the product always has one more end than its author,[111] because every maker is more perfect than what it makes and has some likeness to what it makes.[112] For, just as perpetuity by stages descends from eternity, so temporality by stages descends from perpetuity by becoming inferior. Therefore, just as the first maker is without both ends, so the most remote thing made, which comes about by generation, has both. But because the things in the middle have a beginning by creation or by the first composition, they are without an end. In this way, the things at the extremes are joined together by the things in the middle.

In generated things, however, what they have by creation or by the first composition is not corrupted, but only what they have by generation. [47] For, even if water changes over into a stone, it is, nonetheless, not changed in terms of corporeity, but in terms of the form of aqueousness, and for its form to be corrupted into that is nothing other than for the form of stoneness to be substituted in its place. In every change, it remains the same. I say "the same," however, according to the genus body; it is not the same according to the species water. Hence, the water that was at first and the stone that was made afterwards certainly differ in species, but they wholly agree in the genus of body. For every change of bodies according to generation and corruption comes about only through the form of corporeity. Hence, generation and corruption take place only according to the second genera and according to the third genera and [48] so forth, namely, according to living and sensible and so forth all the way to Socrates.[113] For, because a body does not begin to be a body

---

[111] I am reading *plus* in place of *minus*, because the sense of the passage requires it. Gundissalinus's point, which he makes explicit below, is that God, who is the only eternal being and, thus, the only being with neither a beginning nor an end, has one less end than perpetual creatures, which have a beginning but no end, and that perpetual creatures have one less end than generated creatures, which have both a beginning and an end. Hence, when considering the procession from eternal being to perpetual being to generated being, it is clear that each product in this procession of being has one more end than its author, not one less end.

[112] Avicebron, *Fons vitae* III, 2, p. 76, l. 25: "Every maker makes only what is similar to it."

[113] In a stone, consequently, there is the form of corporeity (*forma corporeitatis*) by virtue of which a stone is a corporeal substance as opposed to an incorporeal substance; there is also in the stone, however, the form of stoneness (*forma lapideitatis*) by virtue of which the stone is a stone as opposed to some other corporeal sub-

by generation, which is a motion of nature, but by the first composition, which is the second motion of the first cause, then every body insofar as it is a body exists perpetually, and every incorporeal substance and whatever began to be by creation or by the first composition is perpetual.[114] Although these are the indivisible works of the Trinity, the creation, nonetheless, of matter, from which all things are made, is attributed to power; the creation of form, by which all things are made, is attributed to wisdom, but the joining of both is fittingly attributed to union so that there is also found a small sign of the Trinity in its first works.

Hence, from the first union of matter and form, only three kinds of things are seen to have proceeded, namely, the invisible creature, celestial bodies, and the four elements. For this reason, these three are perpetual. Therefore, just as [with] the creation of matter and form, so the union of them [49] was not in space or in time, since they are the work of the first cause, which does not operate in time.

Hence, although the first composition comes from things created from nothing, while every composition is posterior to the things out of which it is made, creation, nonetheless, as was said before, preceded composition neither in time nor in order, because it was not in time. But, since the world did not exist as yet, each was made simultaneously in an instant, that is, suddenly. For nothing comes to be in time unless it is understood to have a before and an after. For, according to Aristotle, time is the measure of an interval according to priority and posteriority.[115] Hence, according to others, time is that of which a part has passed and a part is future.[116]

---

stance, such as water or a frog. According to Gundissalinus, then, there is a plurality of forms in any corporeal substance. Though, as I noted in the Introduction, the doctrine of a plurality of forms in creatures has been attributed to Avicebron, from whom Gundissalinus most likely borrowed it, Gundissalinus seems to be thinking of Avicenna, not Avicebron, in the example he gives in the present text. For, in *Physics* I, 2, pp. 18-19, ll. 8-16, Avicenna argues that, although a body such as wax or a portion of water (*pars aquae*) may change with respect to its three dimensions, a body remains a body in relation to its corporeity (*in sua corporeitate*), which is neither changed nor corrupted as the body undergoes change.

[114] Again, only every rational incorporeal substance is perpetual since, as Gundissalinus indicated above, the irrational incorporeal substances, such as sensitive and vegetative souls, can be corrupted.

[115] Although this is Aristotle's definition of time in *Physics* IV, 11, 219a30-b1, Gundissalinus is probably referring, not to Aristotle's *Physics*, but to ibn Ishaq's *On the Heavens and Earth*, which Gundissalinus himself translated and in which—in Chapter 10—Aristotle's definition of time is used to refute other views on the nature of time.

[116] The precise sources are unclear.

Form, however, is simple. But of that which is simple nothing is prior and nothing posterior. Hence, form could not be created in time. But neither could it be united to matter in time. For nothing of it comes before, and nothing of it comes after. But the first composition simultaneously united form to matter in an instant and suddenly. Hence, the composition of the first forms with matter was not in time.

Similarly, the creation of matter from nothing could not come about in time, namely, so that one part of this possibility would, at first, become possible and then another part would come from nothing to possibility. Whatever, however, is not possible was impossible from the first creation of matter. For, if something becomes possible and yet nothing becomes that which it already is, then the impossible becomes possible, [50] which is absurd. Hence, as was said, the possible did not begin to be possible.

Therefore, between matter's being created from nothing and its being formed by additional forms into a corporeal and an incorporeal substance, which is composition, there was no time and sequence. For this and form's being created were simultaneous. Therefore, it is not called formless because it was at some time without form, since all being comes from form, but because it had no form from itself. And therefore, matter never was a substance so that it might be corporeal or incorporeal, although being a substance is prior to being a corporeal or an incorporeal substance. For, in all these cases, when we say "prior," we do not wish to describe a priority in time, but in causality and in diversity of things among themselves, which composition and resolution evidently reveal. In this way, an incorporeal substance, although it is of greater rank, was not, nonetheless, prior to a corporeal substance either in time or in causality since, because they are species of the same genus, they are co-equals. None of them, therefore, began to be a substance prior to the others.

The creation of the angels, therefore, did not precede with respect to time the creation of the celestial bodies or of the elements, or vice versa. Divine Scripture agrees with this where it says: "He who lives eternally created all things simultaneously."[117] Therefore, although Moses first mentioned by name heaven and earth, then light, by which he means the angelic creature, the sequence, nonetheless, [51] in which they are said to have been created is not understood to have existed in their creation. For those things, which went forth into being simultaneously without time, could not be spoken of simultaneously without time. After all, every syllable needs time.

However, since an artisan uses an instrument in acting, certainly there was also an artisan and an instrument in creation and composition. But in generation, mixing, change, and other sorts of composition, which are of second or third rank, the artisan adapted to himself another instrument, that

[117] Sirach 18:1.

is, a secondary cause, so that indeed he made the first things by himself, namely, by creating matter and form from nothing and by combining them with each other, but he entrusted the second and, in order, the third and fourth things to his servant, a secondary cause, to be carried out by its governance and undertaking. Hence, in the beginning there was a twofold cause, namely, a primary and a secondary cause. The primary cause is God; the secondary is his instrument drawn from his very works. But the first are of greater authority than the second.[118]

But the secondary cause is itself a product of the first composition, and all the motions after creation and composition, which are the motions of the first cause, serve it and follow its authority, but at the command of the first cause. Therefore, of secondary causes, which are the instrument of the first cause, the first is the angelic creature, the second is the motion of the heavens, the third is nature, and then the rational soul and some others. For the philosophers say that by the ministry of the angels new souls are created everyday from matter and form, and the celestial souls are also moved.[119]

Moreover, by the motion of the heavens and higher bodies, many things are produced in these lower bodies. For, because the celestial bodies contain [52] these lower bodies within themselves and are contiguous with them and because the higher bodies are always in motion, it is certainly necessary that these bodies be moved according to the motion of them. For, when some large body is moved, it is necessary that a small body that is united to it within it be moved. Since, however, these lower bodies are moved, it is necessary that they be mixed among themselves. But because they have contrary qualities, as happens in every mixture, because that which is stronger acts upon the other, it happens that of the bodies that are produced by the mingling one is said to be hotter or colder or wetter or drier than another from the quality that works more forcefully in the mixture; one is said to be brighter, such as saphire, another darker, such as onyx; and one is prepared to be a receptacle of vegetative life like a plant, another to be receptive of sensitive life like an animal body, and another to be receptive of rational life like a human body. Therefore, because as a result of the motion of the higher bodies these lower bodies are mixed and because from their mixture the different temperaments arise for bodies, the motions of the higher bodies are rightly called a secondary cause.

However, the motion of the higher bodies can do nothing in these lower bodies except by the support of nature. For, using the motion of higher bodies, it acts in some by mixing and changing, as, for example, in congealed things; it nourishes some by attracting, retaining, digesting nutriment, by expelling

---

[118] This paragraph parallels the passage in Hermann of Carinthia, *De essentiis* I, p. 86, ll. 18-29.

[119] The precise sources are unclear.

waste, as, for example, in living things; it moves some by generation, corruption, augmentation, diminution, alteration, and change with respect to place. [53]

Therefore, although there are principally three secondary causes, each, nonetheless, has its own world in which it operates. For the first world, which is beyond the firmament, is incorporeal and incorruptible. The second, which extends from the firmament all the way to the moon, is corporeal and incorruptible. The third, which is lower than the moon, is corporeal and corruptible. Thus, since the first world is insensible and incorruptible while the second is sensible but incorruptible, the third is certainly sensible and corruptible. — Hence, it is truly and properly said about the first world: "He illuminates every man coming into this world,"[120] namely, the first world. We, however, come into this world by the contemplation of the mind, and we are illuminated in it by the knowledge of the truth and the love of virtue. For the human mind ascends, and the divine goodness descends. The mind ascends by contemplation; that goodness descends by revelation.[121]

Its own world is not assigned to the first cause, because it presides everywhere and rules everywhere. It is neither enclosed by a place, nor is it bounded by time. And all other causes do nothing except at its command. On the other hand, with secondary causes, places are assigned to some, times to some, and both places and times to still others so that they are seen to serve under the command of another. For what serves another does not execute its office except when and where the one who presides over it commands.

Therefore, in the first world the first secondary cause receives from the first cause a command concerning all these things that it subsequently brings about in what is lower. In the second world, on the other hand, the second secondary cause receives motion from the first secondary cause in order to move whatever lower thing it touches. In this third world, the third secondary cause [54] operates by various motions insofar as it is commanded by the causes that preside over it. Hence, this sublunar world is truly called by philosophers "the last," because in it nature alone operates according to the command of higher things.[122]

In this way, therefore, the constitution of the whole world proceeded from being nothing to being in possibility, from being in possibility to being in act, and from being in act to corporeal and incorporeal being; and all this happened simultaneously, not in time. For reason required that the institution of the whole world should proceed in this way: namely, that matter and form were,

---

[120] John 1:9.
[121] Hermann of Carinthia, *De essentiis* I: "The human mind ascends; the divine goodness descends. The former by speculation; the latter by revelation" (p. 81).
[122] The precise sources are unclear.

first of all, created from nothing; then, from matter and form the elements and the other things discussed before were composed; and finally, from the mixing and changing of the elements all the things composed of the elements were generated. Reason, that is, required that, first of all, the first simple things should be made from nothing by creation, and that from the simple things composed things should be made by the first union of the simple things, and then that from the composed things the things composed of the elements should be made by generation. And in this way, a progression was made from nothing to simple things, from simple things to composed things, and from composed things to generated things.

Because, therefore, from the first joining of matter and form, three offspring were begotten, namely, the intelligence, the celestial bodies, and the four elements, thus the first cause moves all things, but in a different way. For, some it moves through itself without any means, and some it does not move through itself, but by means of other things. For it principally moves the intelligence through itself without any means. But, according to the philosophers, the intelligences create the souls [55] that move the heavens.[123] The motion of the elements, however, follows from the motion of the heavens. But from the motion of the elements, there comes the mixing of the elements. Their mixing, however, is the procreator of all the things in this lower world.

After all, the most wise creator willed to establish all things according to the order of numbers.[124] For example, just as the number two is placed after unity according to a natural order, so after the first true and simple unity, which is God, two simple unities, which are matter and form, followed in the second place, as if they were the number two. Then, just as the number three is placed in the third place after unity, but second after the number two, so what is composed of matter and form was formed in the third place. Hence, just as the number three is the first number that is indivisible, so the things that are constituted from the union of matter and form alone are incorruptible. Finally, just as the number four comes, in like manner, in the fourth place, so generated things are arranged in the fourth place. And this is rightly so, because, just as the number four admits two divisions—the first into twos and the second into ones—so anything generated is divided first into the elements from which it is entirely composed, and then it is broken down into matter and form as if into the first unities. And just as the number four, which comes in the fourth place, is constituted from four unities, so anything generated is constituted from the four elements as if from four principles. Hence, just as the number three is

---

[123] The precise sources are unclear.

[124] Avicebron, *Fons vitae* IV, 13, p. 239, ll. 12-14: "And in general, when you consider all the things that exist, you will find them ordered and constituted according to the nature of number . . . ."

called "masculine" because it is indivisible and the number four is called "feminine" because it readily admits a multiple division, so a multiple corruption inseparably accompanies generated things. [56]

And every creature exists according to these well-ordered arrangements. Hence, there are four substances in relation to the arrangement of the four numbers. The first of these is the intelligence, which is similar to unity because it apprehends only one thing, namely, the being of a thing, and only one proposition. The second is the rational soul, which is similar to two, because it moves from propositions to a conclusion, from the middle to the end. The sensitive soul, however, is similar to three because it apprehends only a body, which has three dimensions, and it apprehends it by means of three things, namely, color, shape, and motion. Nature, however, is similar to four because, by means of four powers, it operates by four powers and upon everything that is constituted from the four elements.[125]

---

[125] Avicebron, *Fons vitae* IV, 13, p. 239, ll. 5-12: "And I say that the form of the intelligence is similar to the form of one, because it apprehends one proposition. And the form of the rational soul is similar two, because it moves from propositions to a conclusion, from sameness to otherness. And the form of the sensitive soul is similar to three because it apprehends a body, which has three dimensions, by means of three things, which are color, shape, and motion. And the form of nature is similar to four, because nature has four powers."

BIBLIOGRAPHY

PRIMARY SOURCES

Gundissalinus, Dominicus. *Die dem Boethius fälschlich zugeschriebene Abhandlung des Dominicus Gundisalvi "De Unitate."* Herausgegeben und Philosophie-geschichtlich behandelt von Paul Correns. In *Beiträge zur Geschichte der Philosophie des Mittelalters*. Band I. Heft 1. Münster: Aschendorff, 1891.

_____. *Domingo Gundisalvo: De scientiis.* Texto latino establecido por el Manuel Alonso Alonso, S.J. Madrid-Granada, 1954.

_____. *Dominicus Gundissalinus: De divisione philosophiae.* Herausgegeben und Philosophiegeschichtlich untersucht von Ludwig Baur. In *Beiträge zur Geschichte der Philosophie des Mittelalters*. Band IV. Heft 2-3. Münster: Aschendorff, 1903.

_____. *Des Dominicus Gundissalinus Schrift von dem Hervorgange der Welt ("De processione mundi").* Herausgegeben und auf ihre Quellen untersucht von Georg Bülow. In *Beiträge zur Geschichte der Philosophie des Mittelalters*. Band XXIV. Heft 3. Münster: Aschendorff, 1925.

_____. *Des Dominicus Gundissalinus Schrift von der Unsterblichkeit der Seele, nebst einem Anhange, enthaltend die Abhandlung des Wilhelm von Paris "De immortalitate animae."* Herausgegeben und Philosophiegeschichtlich untersucht von Georg Bülow. In *Beiträge zur Geschichte der Philosophie des Mittelalters*. Band II. Heft 3. Münster: Aschendorff, 1897.

_____. *De processione mundi: Estudio y edición crítica del tratado de Domingo Gundisalvo.* Establecido por M. Jesús Soto Bruna y C. Alonso del Real. Pamplona: Ediciones Universidad de Navarra, S.A., 1999.

Muckle, J.T. "The Treatise *De anima* of Dominicus Gundissalinus." *Mediaeval Studies* 2 (1940): 23-103.

SECONDARY SOURCES

Books

Abraham ibn Daud. *The Book of Tradition (Sefer Ha-Qabbalah).* A critical edition, with a Translation and Notes, by Gerson D. Cohen. Philadelphia: The Jewish Publication Society of America, 1967.

_____. *The Exalted Faith.* Translated with Commentary by Norbert M. Samuelson. Translation edited by Gershon Weiss. Cranbury, NJ: Associated University Presses, 1986.

Apuleius. *Opuscules philosophiques (Du dieu de Socrate, Platon et sa doctrine, Du monde) et fragments par Apulée.* Texte etabli, traduit et commenté par Jean Beaujeu. Paris: Les Belles Lettres, 1973.

Avicebron. *Avencebrolis (Ibn Gebirol) Fons Vitae*. Ex arabico in latinvm translatvs ab Iohanne Hispano et Dominico Gvndissalino. Ex codicibvs Parisinis, Amploniano, Colvmbino. Primvm edidit Clemens Baeumker. In *Beiträge zur Geschichte der Philosophie des Mittelalters*. Band I. Heft 2-4. Münster: Aschendorff, 1892-1895.

Avicenna. *Avicenna Latinus: Liber de anima seu Sextus de naturalibus*. Édition critique de la traduction latine médiévale par Simone van Riet. Introduction sur la doctrine psychologique d'Avicenne par G. Verbeke. Louvain: E. Peeters; Leiden: E.J. Brill, 1972.

———. *Avicenna Latinus: Liber de Philosophia Prima sive Scientia Divina*. Édition critique de la traduction latine médiévale par Simone van Riet. Introduction doctrinale par G. Verbeke. Louvain: E. Peeters; Leiden: E.J. Brill, 1977, 1980, 1983.

———. *Avicenna Latinus: Liber primus naturalium: Tractatus primus De causis et principiis naturalium*. Édition critique de la traduction latine médiévale par Simone van Riet. Introduction doctrinale par G. Verbeke. Louvain: E. Peeters; Leiden: E.J. Brill, 1992.

———. *Opera philosophica: Auicène perhypatetici philosophi*. Volume 1. Venice, 1508.

Brunner, Fernand. *Platonisme et Aristotélisme: La critique d'Ibn Gabirol par Saint Thomas d'Aquin*. Louvain: Universitaires de Louvain, 1965.

Cohn-Sherbok, Daniel. *Medieval Jewish Philosophy: An Introduction*. Surrey: Curzon Press, 1996.

Conrad of Prussia. *The Commentary of Conrad of Prussia on the "De unitate et uno" of Dominicus Gundissalinus*. Translated by Joseph Bobik and James A. Corbett. Lewiston, NY: The Edwin Mellen Press, 1989.

De Wulf, Maurice. *Histoire de la philosophie médiévale*. Tome deuxième. Sixième édition. Louvain: Institut Supérieur de Philosophie; Paris: J. Vrin, 1936.

Gilson, Étienne. *History of Christian Philosophy in the Middle Ages*. London: Sheed and Ward, 1955.

González Palencia, C.A. *Los mozárabes de Toledo en los siglos XII y XIII*. Tomo I. Madrid: Mestre, 1926.

Guttmann, Jacob. *Die Religions-philosophie des Abraham ibn Daud aus Toledo*. Göttingen, 1879.

Guy, Alain. *Histoire de la philosophie espagnole*. Deuxième édition. Toulouse: Association des Publications de l'Université de Toulouse-Le Mirail, 1985.

Hermann of Carinthia. *Hermann of Carinthia: De essentiis*. A critical edition, with Translation and Commentary, by Charles Burnett. Leiden: E.J. Brill, 1982.

Husik, Isaac. *A History of Mediaeval Jewish Philosophy*. Philadelphia: The Jewish Publication Society of America, 1946.

Luis Abellán, José. *Historia crítica del pensamiento español*. Tomo I. Madrid: Espasa-Calpe, S.A., 1979.

McInerny, Ralph M. *A History of Western Philosophy*. Volume 2. Notre Dame, IN: University of Notre Dame Press, 1970.

Munk, Solomon. *Mélanges de philosophie juive et arabe*. Nouvelle édition. Paris: J. Vrin, 1955.

Porphyry. *Isagoge*. Translated by Edward W. Warren. Toronto: The Pontifical Institute of Mediaeval Studies, 1975.

Sarton, George. *Introduction to the History of Science*. Volume 2. Part 2. London, 1931.

Selk, Eugene Edward. *The Meaning of the Formula 'omne esse ex forma est' in the De Processione Mundi of Dominicus Gundissalinus.* M.A. Thesis. Marquette University, 1966.

Sirat, Colette. *La philosophie juive au moyen âge.* Paris: Centre National de la Recherche Scientifique, 1983.

William of Auvergne. *The Immortality of the Soul (De immortalitate animae).* Translated from the Latin, with an Introduction and Notes, by Roland J. Teske, S.J. Milwaukee: Marquette University Press, 1991.

Articles and Chapters in Books

Alonso Alonso, S.J., Manuel. "Domingo Gundisalvo y el *De causis primis et secundis.*" *Estudios eclesiásticos* 21 (1947): 367-380.

_____. "Las fuentes literarias de Domingo Gundisalvo." *Al-Andalus* 11 (1946): 159-173.

_____. "Gundisalvi y el *Tractatus de anima.*" *Pensamiento* 4 (1948): 71-77.

_____. "Hugo de San Victor refutado por Domingo Gundisalvo hacia el 1170." *Estudios eclesiásticos* 21 (1947): 209-216.

_____. "Notas sobre los traductores toledanos Domingo Gundisalvo y Juan Hispano." In *Temas filosoficos medievales: Ibn Dawud y Gundisalvo.* Comillas: Pontificia Universitas Comillensis, 1959.

_____. "Las traducciones del Arcediano Domingo Gundisalvo." *Al-Andalus* 12 (1947): 295-338.

Aubert, R. "Gundisalvi (Dominique), Gundissalinus, Gondisalvi." In *Dictionnaire d'histoire et de géographie ecclésiastique.* Volume 22. Paris: Letouzey et Ané, 1988.

Baeumker, Clemens. "Les écrits philosophiques de Dominicus Gundissalinus." *Revue thomiste* 5 (1897): 723-745.

Bédoret, S.J., H. "Les premières versions tolédanes de philosophie: Œuvres d'Avicenne." *Revue néoscolastique de philosophie* 41 (1938): 374-400.

Brasa Diez, O.P., Mariano. "Traducciones y traductores toledanos." *Estudios filosboficos* 23 (1974): 129-137.

D'Alverny, M. T. "Avicenna Latinus." *Archives d'histoire doctrinale et littéraire du moyen âge* 27-28 (1960-1961): 281-316.

_____. "Dominic Gundisalvi (Gundissalinus)." In *The New Catholic Encyclopedia.* Volume 4. New York: McGraw-Hill, 1967.

_____. "Notes sur les traductions médiévales d'Avicenne." *Archives d'histoire doctrinale et littéraire du moyen âge* 19 (1952): 337-358.

De Vaux, O.P., Roland. "La fin du *De anima* de Gundissalinus." In *Notes et textes sur l'Avicennisme latin aux confins des XIIe-XIIIe siècles.* Paris: J. Vrin, 1934.

Diaz Diaz, Gonzalo. "Domingo Gundisalvo." In *Hombres y documentos de la filsofia española.* Volume 2. Madrid: Consejo Superior de Investigaciones Cientificas, 1983.

_____. "Juan Hispano." In *Hombres y documentos de la filsofia española.* Volume 4. Madrid: Consejo Superior de Investigaciones Cientificas, 1991.

García Fayós, J. "El colegio de traductores de Toledo y Domingo Gundisalvo." *Revista de la Biblioteca, Archivo y Museo* 33 (1932): 109-123.

Guttmann, Jacob. "Abraham Ibn Daud (=David) Ha-Levi." In *The Jewish Encyclopaedia.* Volume 1. New York: Ktav Publishing House, 1901.

Hugonnard-Roche, Henri. "La classification des sciences de Gundissalinus et l'influence d'Avicenne." In *Études sur Avicenne*. Dirigées par Jean Jolivet et Roshdi Rashed. Paris: Société d'Édition Les Belles Lettres, 1984.

Jolivet, Jean. "The Arabic Inheritance." In *A History of Twelfth-Century Western Philosophy*. Edited by Peter Dronke. Cambridge: Cambridge University Press, 1988.

Kren, Claudia. "Gundissalinus, Dominicus." In *Dictionary of Scientific Biography*. Volume 5. Edited by Charles Coulston Gillispie. New York: Charles Scribner's Sons, 1972.

Laumakis, John A. "Weisheipl's Interpretation of Avicebron's Doctrine of the Divine Will: Is Avicebron a Voluntarist?" Forthcoming in the *American Catholic Philosophical Quarterly*.

Mansilla, D. "La documentación pontificia del archivo de la Catedral de Burgos." *Hispania sacra* 1 (1948): 141-162.

Puig, Josep. "The Transmission and Reception of Arabic Philosophy in Christian Spain (Until 1200)." In *The Introduction of Arabic Philosophy into Europe*. Edited by Charles E. Butterworth and Blake Andrée Kessel. Leiden: E.J. Brill, 1994.

Saffrey, O.P., H.D. "Gondisalvi ou Gundisalvi (Dominique)." In *Catholicisme*. Tome cinquième. Paris: Letouzey et Ané, 1963.

INDEX OF NAMES

INDEX OF TERMS

MEDIÆVAL PHILOSOPHICAL TEXTS IN TRANSLATION
COMPLETE LIST

UNDER THE EDITORSHIP OF GERARD SMITH, SJ

Grosseteste. *On Light*. Clare Riedl, Tr. ISBN 0-87462-201-8 (Translation No. 1, 1942). 28 pp. $5.

St. Augustine. *Against the Academicians*. Mary Patricia Garvey, R.S.M., Tr. ISBN 0-87462-202-6. (Translation No. 2, 1942). 94 pp. $10

Pico Della Mirandola. *Of Being and Unity*. Victor M. Hamm, Tr. ISBN 0-87462-203-4. (Translation No. 3, 1943). 40 pp. $10

Francis Suarez. *On the Various Kinds of Distinctions*. Cyril Vollert, SJ, Tr. ISBN 0-87462-204-2. (Translation No. 4, 1947). 72 pp. $10

St. Thomas Aquinas. *On Spiritual Creatures*. Mary C. Fitzpatrick, Tr. ISBN 0-87462-205-0. (Translation No. 5, 1949). 144 pp. $15

Guigo. *Meditations of Guigo*. John J. Jolin, SJ, Tr. ISBN 0-87462-206-9. (Translation No. 6, 1951). 96 pp. $10

Giles of Rome. *Theorems on Existence and Essence*. Michael V. Murray, SJ, Tr. ISBN 0-87462-207-7. (Translation No. 7, 1953). 128 pp. $15

John of St. Thomas. *Outlines of Formal Logic*. Francis C. Wade, SJ, Tr. ISBN 0-87462-208-5. (Translation No. 8, 1955). 144 pp. $15

Hugh of St. Victor. *Soliloquy in the Earnest Money of the Soul*. Kevin Herbert, Tr. ISBN 0-87462-209-3. (Translation No. 9, 1956). 48 pp. $5

UNDER THE EDITORSHIP OF JAMES H. ROBB

St. Thomas Aquinas. *On Charity*. Lottie Kendzierski, Tr. ISBN 0-87462-210-7. (Translation No. 10, 1960). 120 pp. $15

Aristotle. *On Interpretation*. *Commentary by St. Thomas and Cajetan*. Jean T. Oesterle, Tr. ISBN 0-87462-211-5. (Translation No. 11, 1962). 288 pp. $20

Desiderius Erasmus of Rotterdam. *On Copia of Words and Ideas*. Donald B. King and H. David Rix, Tr. ISBN 0-87462-212-3. (Translation No. 12, 1963). 124 pp. $15

Peter of Spain. *Tractatus Syncategorematum and Selected Anonymous Treatises*. Joseph P. Mullally and Roland Houde, Tr. ISBN 0-87462-213-1. (Translation No. 13, 1964). 168 pp. $15

Cajetan. *Commentary on St. Thomas Aquinas' On Being and Essence*. Lottie Kendzierski and Francis C. Wade, SJ, Tr. ISBN 0-87462-214-X. (Translation No. 14, 1965). 366 pp. $20

Suárez. *Disputation VI, On Formal and Universal Unity*. James F. Ross, Tr. ISBN 0-87462-215-8. (Translation. No. 15, 1965). 132 pp. $15

St. Thomas, Siger de Brabant, St. Bonaventure. *On the Eternity of the World*. Cyril Vollert, SJ, Lottie Kendzierski, and Paul Byrne, Tr. ISBN 0-87462-216-6. (Translation No. 16, 1965). 132 pp. $15

Geoffrey of Vinsauf. *Instruction in the Method and Art of Speaking and Versifying.* Roger P. Parr, Tr. ISBN 0-87462-217-4. (Translation No. 17, 1968). 128 pp. $15

Liber De Pomo. *The Apple, or Aristotle's Death.* Mary F. Rousseau, Tr. ISBN 0-87462-218-2. (Translation No. 18, 1968). 96 pp. $5

St. Thomas Aquinas. *On the Unity of the Intellect against the Averroists.* Beatrice H. Zedler, Tr. ISBN 0-87462-219-0. (Translation No. 19, 1969). 96 pp. $10

Nicholas of Autrecourt. *The Universal Treatise.* Leonard L. Kennedy, CSB., Tr. ISBN 0-87462-220-4. (Translation No. 20, 1971). 174 pp. $15

Pseudo-Dionysius Areopagite. *The Divine Names and Mystical Theology.* John D. Jones, Tr. ISBN 0-87462-221-2. (Translation No. 21, 1980). 320 pp. $25

Matthew of Vendome. *Ars Versificatoria.* Roger P. Parr, Tr. ISBN 0-87462-222-0. (Translation No. 22, 1981). 150 pp. $15

Francis Suárez. *On Individuation.* Jorge J.E. Gracia, Tr. ISBN 0-87462-223-9. (Translation No. 23, 1982). 304 pp. $35

Francis Suárez. *On the Essence of Finite Being as Such, on the Existence of That Essence and Their Distinction.* Norman J. Wells, Tr. ISBN 0-87462-224-7. (Translation No. 24, 1983). 248 pp. $20

The Book of Causes (Liber De Causis). Dennis J. Brand, Tr. ISBN 0-87462-225-5. (Translation No. 25, 1984). 56 pp. $7.50

Giles of Rome. *Errores Philosophorum.* John O. Riedl, Tr. Intro. by Josef Koch. ISBN 0-87462-429-0. (Translation No. 26, 1944). 136 pp. $10

St. Thomas Aquinas. *Questions on the Soul.* James H. Robb, Tr. ISBN 0-87462-226-3. (Translation No. 27, 1984). 285 pp. $25

UNDER THE EDITORSHIP OF RICHARD C. TAYLOR

William of Auvergne. *The Trinity.* Roland J. Teske, SJ and Francis C. Wade, SJ ISBN 0-87462-231-X (Translation No. 28, 1989) 286 pp. $20

UNDER THE EDITORSHIP OF ROLAND J. TESKE, SJ

Hugh of St. Victor. *Practical Geometry.* Frederick A. Homann, SJ, Tr. ISBN 0-87462-232-8 (Translation No. 29, 1991) 92 pp. $10

William of Auvergne. *The Immortality of the Soul.* Roland J. Teske, SJ, Tr. ISBN 0-87462-233-6 (Translation No. 30, 1992) 72 pp. $10

Dietrich of Freiberg. *Treatise of the Intellect and the Intelligible.* M. L. Führer, Tr. ISBN 0-87462-234-4 (Translation No. 31, 1992) 135 pp. $15

Henry of Ghent. *Quodlibetal Questions on Free Will.* Roland J. Teske, SJ, Tr. ISBN 0-87462-234-4 (Translation No. 32, 1993) 135 pp. $15

Francisco Suárez, SJ. *On Beings of Reason. Metaphysical Disputation LIV.* John P. Doyle, Tr. ISBN 0-87462-236-0 (Translation No. 33, 1995) 170 pp. $20

Francisco De Vitoria, OP. *On Homicide,* and *Commentary on Thomas Aquinas. Summa theologiae IIaIIae, 64.* Edited and Translated by John Doyle. ISBN 0-87462-237-9. (Translation No. 34, 1997) 280 pp. $30

William of Auvergne. *The Universe of Creatures*. Edited, Translated, and with an Introduction by Roland J. Teske, SJ. ISBN 0-87462-238-7 (Translation No. 35, 1998) 235 pp. $25

Francis Suarez, SJ. *On the Formal Cause of Substance. Metaphysical Disputation XV.* Translated by John Kronen & Jeremiah Reedy. Introduction & Explanatory Notes by John Kronen. ISBN 0-87462-239-5 (Translation No. 36, 2000) 218 pp. $25

William of Auvergne. *The Soul*. Translated from the Latin with an Introduction and Notes by Roland J. Teske, SJ. ISBN 0-87462-240-9 (Translation No. 37, 2000) 516 pp. $50

The Conimbricenses. Some Questions on Signs. Translated with Introduction and Notes by John P. Doyle. ISBN 0-87462-241-7 (Translation No. 38, 2001) 217 pp. $25

Dominicus Gundissalinus. *The Procession of the World (De processione mundi)*. Translated from the Latin with an Introduction & Notes by John A. Laumakis. ISBN 0-87462-242-5 (Translation No. 39, 2002) 87 pp. $10

Francisco Suárez. *A Commentary on Aristotle's Metaphysics or "A Most Ample Index to the Metaphysics of Aristotle" (Index locupletissimus in Metaphysicam Aristotelis)*. Translated with an Introduction & Notes by John P. Doyle. ISBN 0-87462-243-3 (Translation No. 40, 2003) 430 pp. $45

Henry of Ghent. *Quodlibetal Question on Moral Problems*. Translated from the Latin with an Introduction and Notes by Roland J. Teske, SJ. ISBN 0-87462-244-1 (Translation No. 41, 2005) 82 pp. $10

Francisco Suárez. *On Real Relation (Disputatio Metaphysica XLVII)* A Translation from the Latin, with an Introduction and Notes by John P. Doyle. ISBN 978-0-87462-244-1 (Translation No. 42, 2006) 430 pp. $45

William of Auvergne. *The Providence of God Regarding the Universe. Part Three of the First Principal Part of The Universe of Creatures*. Translated from the Latin with an Introduction and Notes by Roland J. Teske, SJ. ISBN 978-0-87462-246-1 (Translation No. 43, 2007) 204 pp. $23

Hervaeus Natalis. *A Treatise of Master Hervaeus Natalis, The Doctor Perspicacissimus, On Second Intentions. Volume One—An English Translation & Volume Two—A Latin Edition* by John P. Doyle. ISBN 978-0-87462-247-8 (Translation No. 44, 2008) 622 pp. $47

William of Auvergne. *On the Virtues: Part One of On the Virtues and Vices [De virtutibus et vitiis]*. Translated from the Latin and with an Introduction and Notes by Roland J. Teske, SJ. ISBN 978-0-87462-248-5 (Translation No. 45, 2009) 310 pp. $30

Albertus, Magnus. *On the Causes of the Properties of the Elements [Liber de causis proprietatum elementorum)*. Translated by Irven M. Resnick. ISBN 978-0-87462-249-2 (Translation no. 46, 2010) 132 pp. $15

Gottschalk and a Medieval Predestination Controversy: Texts Translated from the Latin. Edited & Translated by Victor Genke & Francis X. Gumerlock with an Introduction by Victor Genke. ISBN 978-0-87462-253-9 (Translation No. 47, 2010) 246 pp. $29

Henry of Ghent's Summa of Ordinary Questions. Articles Six to Ten on Theology. Translated & Annotated by Roland J. Teske, SJ. ISBN 978-0-87462-255-3 (Translation No. 48, 2011) 221 pp. $25

Henry of Ghent's Summa of Ordinary Questions. Articles Thirty-one & Thirty-two, on God's Eternity & the Divine Attributes in General. Translated & annotated by Roland J. Teske, SJ. ISBN 978-0-87462-257-7 (Translation No. 49, 2012) 144 pp. $17

Henry of Ghent's Summa of Ordinary Questions. Articles 35, 36, 41, 45. Translated & annotated by Roland J. Teske, SJ. ISBN 978-0-87462-259-1 (Translation No. 50, 2013) 184 pp. $20

Solomon ibn Gabirol (Avicebron) *The Font of Life (Fons vitae).* Translated from the Latin with an Introduction by John A. Laumakis. ISBN 978-0-87462-261-4 (Translation No. 51, 2014) 281 pp. $29

Henry of Ghent's Summa of Ordinary Questions. Articles 53-55, On the Divine Persons Translated & annotated by Roland J. Teske, SJ. ISBN 978-0-87462-263-8 (Translation No. 52, 2015) 330 pp. $29

MEDIÆVAL PHILOSOPHICAL TEXTS IN TRANSLATION
ROLAND J. TESKE, SJ, EDITOR

This series originated at Marquette University in 1942, and with revived interest in Mediæval studies is read internationally with steadily increasing popularity. Available in attractive, durable, colored soft covers. Volumes priced from $5 to $50 each. Complete Set [0-87462-200-X] receives a 40% discount. John Riedl's *A Catalogue of Renaissance Philosophers*, hardbound with red cloth, is an ideal reference companion title (sent free with purchase of complete set). New standing orders receive a 20% discount and a free copy of the Riedl volume. Regular reprinting keeps all volumes available. Recent volumes are also available as ebooks.

See our web page: http://www.marquette.edu/mupress/
Order from:
    Marquette University Press
    30 Amberwood Parkway
    Ashland OH 44805
    Tel. 800-247-6553 Fax: 419-281-6883

Editorial Address for Mediæval Philosophical Texts in Translation:
    Department of Philosophy
    Marquette University
    Box 1881
    Milwaukee WI 53201-1881

Marquette University Press office:
    Marquette University Press
    Box 3141
    Milwaukee WI 53201-3141
    Tel: (414) 288-1564
    www.marquette.edu/mupress/

Printed in the United States
By Bookmasters